Welcome...
...to a new lifestyle!

Your own home from home in your favourite location. A haven of tranquillity. Fabulous views from your windows. A beach a stone's throw away. Woodland walks on your doorstep. A bolthole from work-school-commuting routine, a place in which you can relax, away from the inevitable house and garden chores. A place in which all the family spends quality time in one, spacious, open-plan living area. A quiet park that's a true get-away-from-it-all environment. Or a full-on family fun park where the activity only stops for bedtime...

Whatever your idea of what holiday home ownership means, it will enrich your lives immensely.

Tempted? Go for it! Splash some cash and you will reap huge rewards however you prefer to spend your leisure time. Along the journey, from your first thought that a holiday home might be a good idea, to getting the keys, this magazine will guide you all of the way.

Our advice section guides you on how to choose the right park and right home for you, on prices and ongoing costs, on insurance, on heating... it's all here and more.

We have reviewed some of the most gorgeous holiday homes for you, and beautiful parks, too – more than 40 in total.

And there's more help and advice along the way to your new lifestyle. Buying Your Holiday Home's sister magazine, Park and Holiday Home Inspiration, is an on-going source of info – as well as inspiration – and so is our website, outandaboutlive.co.uk.

SIGN UP TO OUR EMAIL NEWSLETTER!
If you want to be the first to hear the latest news and read our most recent reviews, make sure you sign up to *Park & Holiday Home Inspiration*'s email newsletter. You will also receive updates and launch details from carefully selected manufacturers and parks. Go to outandaboutlive.co.uk/account/create

VAL CHAPMAN
EDITOR

Imagine... A view like this from your holiday home park (page 110)

Imagine.... Your new adventure – and loads of family fun (page 66)

Imagine.. Your holiday home in a nature lovers' paradise (page 58)

Imagine... A holiday home like this ... (the Alderney, from Omar, page 28)

Or this... (the Tamarack, from Oakgrove, page 46)

Or this one... (the Ashurst, from Willerby, page 16)

PARK & HOLIDAY HOME Inspiration

Warners Group Publications plc
The Maltings, West Street,
Bourne, Lincolnshire PE10 9PH
T 01778 391000
E phhi@warnersgroup.co.uk
W outandaboutlive.co.uk/lodges

MANAGEMENT
Publisher Fleur Chivers
Managing Director Stephen Warner

EDITOR
Val Chapman

DESIGN
Designers Sarah Machin, Nicola Lang
Advertising Designer Viv Lane

MARKETING
Brand Manager Lucie Cox
T 01778 395016
E luciec@warnersgroup.co.uk

ADVERTISING
Head of Advertising
Ashleigh Chadwick T 01778 392050
Account Manager
Connor Jackson T 01778 392057
Production
Kate Goulding T 01778 391104

SUBSCRIBE
Get *Park & Holiday Home Inspiration* discounted. For our latest offers, contact 01778 392490 or visit outandaboutlive.co.uk/lodges/store/subscriptions

WARNERS GROUP PUBLICATIONS
PRINTED BY WARNERS MIDLANDS PLC LINCOLNSHIRE PE10 9PH
We are not responsible for the quality and/or performance of goods and/or services advertised. The Advertising Standards Authority (ASA) exists to regulate the content of advertisements and can be contacted on 020 7492 2222.

Park & Holiday Home Inspiration is published 6 times a year by Warners Group plc
© Copyright 2020 Warners Group plc

DOWNLOAD THIS ISSUE
Visit *bit.ly/1R8RrPj*

World of Park & Leisure Homes Shows

 FREE ENTRY   **FREE** PARKING   **FREE** SHOWGUIDE

A massive display of Homes to view including the latest models and designs. Plus, information on hundreds of Sites arounds the UK and beyond, experts on hand to offer help and guidance and a range of selected companies providing the latest accessories, services and products for these wonderful homes. It's your chance to discover this affordable and fabulous leisure lifestyle.

Don't miss the South of Englands biggest Park and Leisure Home show

South of England Showground, Ardingly, West Sussex, RH17 6TL
Friday 3rd — Sunday 5th April 2020
Trade preview day Thursday 2nd April

NEW for 2020 World of Pods

2 Fantastic Shows

NAEC Stoneleigh, Stoneleigh Park Warwickshire, CV8 2TA
Friday 12th — Sunday 14th June 2020
Trade preview day Thursday 11th June

Don't miss the UK's biggest dedicated Park and Leisure Homes show

more homes, more traders, the best deals and they're **FREE** to enter
The UK's leading shows for Park & leisure Homes
www.parkhomeandleisure.co.uk

CONTENTS

16 Holiday homes for all tastes and wallets

62 Your new adventure!

82 Seaside splendour on the Gower Peninsula in Wales

6 Your new leisure lifestyle starts here
All you need to know about buying a holiday home

16 Holiday homes for all tastes and wallets
We review four homes from the Willerby collection

20 Bee a member!
Buyers of Willerby homes are invited to join a club

23 Luxury in country style
Three country-style lodges from Wessex

28 Lodges in three very different styles
Luxury, mid-range and compact lodges from Omar

32 Exceptional opportunities!
Pathfinder homes on exclusive parks in the southwest

36 Amazing designs!
Five spectacular lodges from the Tingdene range

41 10 things to consider when buying
Our at-a-glance guide to buying your first holiday home

42 Sophisticated and spacious
A lodge with up to four bedrooms from Oakgrove

46 Spring plans for The Springs!
New holiday homes in Worcestershire

50 Mortgageable holiday homes
At Aria Resorts, lodges on which you can take a mortgage

54 Lodges with hot tubs in Cornwall
Sheltered by dunes and close to a beach

58 Natural Norfolk
A park in 300 acres of heathland and woodland

62 Your new adventure
Parkdean Resorts has 62 parks – pick yours!

66 A holiday that's ready whenever you are
Homes in eight locations from Club Holiday Homes

70 A complete family resort in Norfolk
An array of facilities, eateries and entertainment

74 Tranquillity and nature
Five miles from Southport, a park where nature is key

78 Coast and country escapes for families
Seaside, lakeside and forest locations from Away Resorts

82 Seaside splendour in Wales
On the Gower Peninsula, with views of the sea

86 Quiet quality in Kent
Three parks, all with different characters

88 Family heritage on the Suffolk coast
Cales & Ale – a park with an intriguing name and history

90 Escape, relax and enjoy!
New and pre-owned homes close to the Cornish coast

92 Discover something spectacular!
Exceptional luxury lodges in a lakeside setting

94 Your place in Constable country...
... with views that inspired the artist, John Constable

96 A holiday home on a farm
In Somerset, close to the coast and with a lovely view

98 A canalside centre of activity
In the Staffordshire countryside; plenty for families to do

100 A haven in the Peak District
A brilliant centre for family activities

102 Devon delight!
New lodges on a park with a restaurant, bar and pool

104 Beautiful southwest borderlands
On the Devon-Cornwall border, a small, peaceful park

106 Yorkshire tranquillity
Two parks in moorland and hill locations

108 Natural north Devon
A 33-acre park in its own secluded valley

110 Gadgets and gizmos
You're sure to love these smart devices

114 A new lodge development in Scotland
Close to the oldest golf course in the world

ADVICE

YOUR NEW LEISURE LIFESTYLE STARTS HERE

From idea to dream come true – all you need to know about buying a holiday home

Image Willerby

Words **Val Chapman**

Buying a holiday home starts you out on a new lifestyle. Finding your perfect home and ideal location is intensely exciting, and it can seem also a little daunting – until you know more. That's where this magazine comes in. Let us be your guide every step of the journey, from the first thought that you might like your own home from home in which to spend your leisure time, to stepping inside your dream holiday home. So, where do you start?

Let us take you through the journey to owning a holiday home. It's tempting to start by being wowed by gorgeous holiday homes online, in brochures – and in this magazine. That's the glossy bit – and, in many senses, the easiest bit. You need to do some detailed foundation work, though – first, to make sure you buy your holiday home in the right place... Your guide starts here!

At a glance factors to consider

- ❏ The location
- ❏ The park
- ❏ Holiday home or lodge – what's the difference?
- ❏ Standard of insulation and heating
- ❏ Your budget
- ❏ Costs involved
- ❏ How to choose the best holiday home for you
- ❏ Dogs!

The right location

Most families and couples who buy holiday homes choose a park which is within two hours – or in some cases a lot less – of their home. That way, you can get there on a Friday evening after work and arrive in time for dinner.

Not having a long distance to travel means you can use your holiday home more often. And, if you're considering fuel cost, it also means that each visit costs you less than if you were driving a long distance.

It's very tempting to dream of owning a holiday home on the south coast, for example. But, if you live in the Midlands or further north, the reality is that you won't get there as often as you would like, simply because of travel time.

You also might like to consider the type of journey to your holiday home location. If it's possible to avoid routes that are known to become traffic-choked, that will also avoid frustration, and will ensure that, as far as is possible, you know your arrival time – and you also know how long it will take you to get home at the end of your stay.

So, step one: Draw a 'two-hour circle' around your home and begin to explore what holiday home parks there are in that area.

Woodland walks are a favourite family pastime for holidays and weekends away in a holiday home

Take to the road – at a leisurely pace – another top favourite family activity

Image Willerby

What's in the area

Do you enjoy walking? Cycling? Golf? Fishing? Tennis? Going to a gym? Consider an area that offers things that match up with your pursuits of choice. And if walking and cycling are your preferences, consider the terrain. Do you want challenging cycling? Off-road or road? Is your style of walking a full-on hill expedition, or an afternoon stroll with a coffee shop en route? Do you enjoy spending time in towns or cities? Eating? Shopping? Exploring historical interest?

By considering all of these things you will quickly begin to build a picture of your ideal location.

ADVICE
The right park for you

Full-on family fun? Or quiet and remote? Each park has its own character and its facilities play a big part in creating that.

Do you want a location in which you can escape from the realities of work life for a while? Somewhere quiet, where the only sound is birdsong and breeze rustling through leaves. It's an enticing prospect – just arrive, relax and unwind in your own home from home…

Much will depend on whether you're a couple or whether you have a family, of course. Or maybe you're a couple with a 'part-time' family – grandchildren who may come and share your holiday home retreat on an occasional basis.

Do you prefer a park where the focus is firmly on family fun? A swimming pool, a restaurant, play areas, entertainment, perhaps. Somewhere to which the kids are going to be really excited to go, for things they can't do at home. And that, after all, is the essence of holiday home ownership – a home where life is different from that at your main home, however you define it.

Between the two extremes of tranquillity and family focus there is a large choice of types of park. What suits you is so individual – and, until you begin to research, and then visit parks, you may not have a clear idea of what suits you. Sometimes, a park just feels 'right', in an indefinable way.

Now it's time to look at individual parks, and to draw up a shortlist. Maybe three, or four. Then go and visit – more than once. One of those visits should ideally be on a rainy day – because, if a park still appeals to you in the inevitable reality of rain, then the chances are you will be happy there. Also, if you're starting your search at any other time than summer, see what the park looks like when there are no leaves on the trees. If it still looks good then, it's a very good-looking park.

Fishing on the Avon, at Stratford Parks, three holiday parks a mile from Stratford-upon-Avon

Adventure play is a great way to make friends

Image **Parkdean Resorts**

If you want to pick a park with a restaurant you will find there are plenty. This is Riverside Park in Stratford

" The essence of holiday home ownership is a place where life is different from that at your main home, however you define it "

ADVICE
All year or most of the year

Some holiday parks are open all year. Others close for a period of between two weeks and four months.
This is a major influencing factor. There is a distinct difference between the holiday home lifestyle in summer and winter. Summer equals barbecues and sitting in the sun. Winter equals cosy evenings in, with television and music as your focus. Both can be equally special. If you want to be able to use your home at all times of the year, pick a park that doesn't close, or which closes for a minimal period of time.

For some parks, the closure period doesn't involve Christmas. That's something to consider when you are picking a park, if you fancy spending some Christmases in your holiday home. Maybe it's an ideal place for a family gathering. Maybe you want Christmas in seclusion. Either way, it's important!

An example of a lodge – this is ABI's Harrogate

Holiday home or lodge – what's the difference?

Holiday home? Static caravan? Lodge? What do these terms mean? It's a fair question...

First: lodge. That's straightforward. A lodge is almost always what is termed a double-width unit – that's usually 20 feet wide. It's in the luxury category with a price to match. Something to consider if you are going to be spending a great deal of your time in your holiday home, so it's worth buying a large unit with lots of luxury.

The distinction between the terms 'holiday home' and 'static caravan' is slightly obscure. That's because of two factors. At one time, all caravans which were not designed to be towed were called 'statics'. Then, in the 1980s and 1990s, the marketeers got hold of the static caravan concept and decided the term 'static' should be replaced by 'holiday home', deemed to make them sound more appealing. So the industry switched its terminology. Then the internet arrived and, with it, the concept of key words. People search for 'statics'; the term 'holiday home' can

10 | Buying Your First Holiday Home 2020

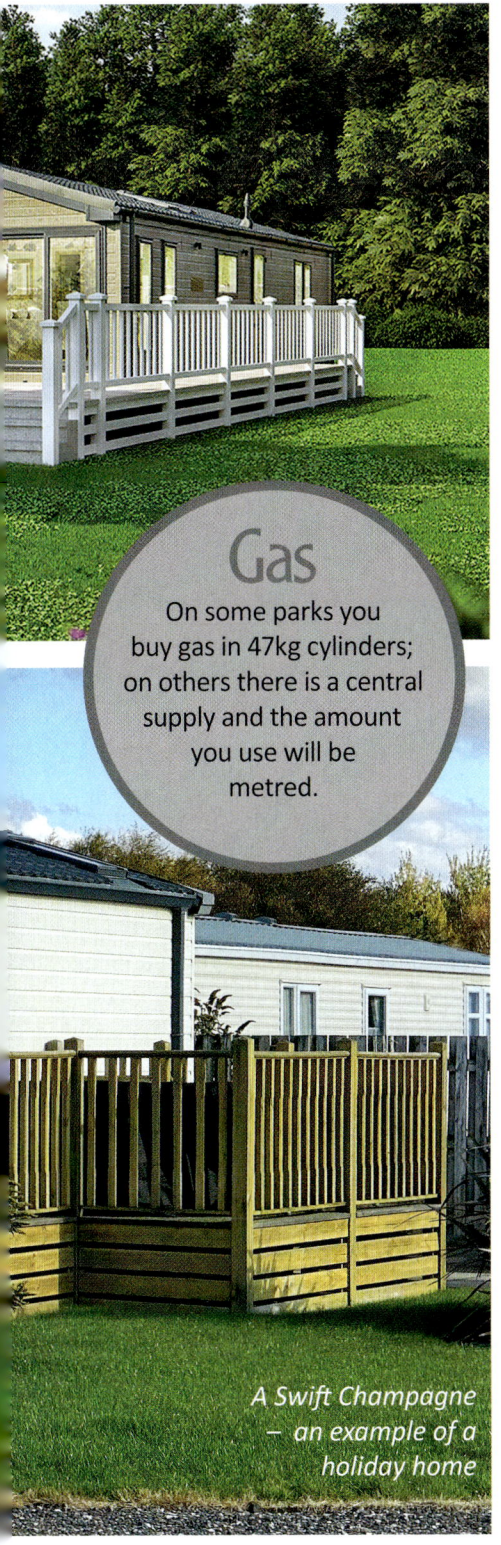

Gas
On some parks you buy gas in 47kg cylinders; on others there is a central supply and the amount you use will be metred.

A Swift Champagne – an example of a holiday home

mean a stone cottage or an apartment – anything that's not your main residence. So the term 'static' remains alive and well and online, at least!

Holiday homes are usually 12-14ft wide and 28-40ft long or more.

Both lodges and holiday homes have either two or three bedrooms and a few have four.

Standards of insulation and heating

Before we take you any further on the journey to finding your perfect holiday home, allow us to clarify one factor. Thoughts of using your holiday home in winter provoke thoughts of heating – and standards of insulation.

Most holiday homes are centrally heated, in much the same way as a domestic home. For those which don't have central heating as standard, it's an option. Many holiday homes are constructed to residential standard, which means their level of insulation is suitable for use at any time of the year. For some others, it's possible to upgrade to residential standard at the time you place your order. That's, in official terms, Residential Specification BS 3632: 2015.

The official standard for holiday homes is EN 1647. This is the European standard for static caravan holiday homes. Models built to this standard are usually intended for seasonal use.

Holiday homes built to BS 3632 standard have residential standards of insulation to all walls, the floor and the roof.

How much to budget for…

Anything from £15,000 to £250,000 and more… Puzzled? When you break it down, it's not puzzling at all.

You can buy a pre-owned holiday home for around £15,000 or less. That's a good place to start. You can then, perhaps, upgrade to a new one after a few years. That's when you've settled into the leisure-home-versus-main residence routine and discovered exactly how much time you are spending at your leisure home – and therefore how much it's worth investing in upgrading. New holiday homes start at around £23,000 and climb in price commensurate with level of luxury as well as size.

The amount you pay for a particular new holiday home is governed by the park it is on. That's for three reasons.

The first is location. A park in a prime location will charge more for holiday homes because demand is high and people are prepared to pay more to get a leisure home in that location.

The second is the park's facilities. The more facilities, the higher the cost, as the park needs to recoup its costs in providing those facilities.

The third is about transport and siting costs. Often these are included in the purchase price. So, too, will be connection to mains and waste water services and to the park's electricity supply. In some cases skirting around the base of the home, and also decking, may be included. Decking gives you steps up to the door and a patio area at the front and/or side.

ADVICE

Ladram Bay Holiday Park, on the south Devon coast, is one which has a sublet scheme – and its own beach
Image: Richard Chapman

What influences pitch or plot fees

The vast majority of holiday home parks charge an annual fee for the pitch that your holiday home occupies. The rare exceptions are a few parks on which you actually purchase the freehold of the land on which your holiday home sits.

Pitch or plot (as they are sometimes called) fees vary widely. There are two factors. Just like price of holiday homes, one is location; the other is the facilities on the park. The influence of location is all about what the area offers. If the park is in an area which is not regarded as a holiday region, the plot fees are going to be lower than on a park in a prime holiday location such as Dorset, Devon and the Lake District.

And facilities? If the park has a swimming pool, a restaurant complex and other attractions, the plot fee is likely to be higher than on a park with minimal facilities. As a rough guide, expect to pay between £1,500 and £6,000 a year; more for parks with an exceptional array of facilities.

Why insurance is important

Just like any other major purchase, insurance is vital. Indeed, park operators insist that you provide, on an annual basis, proof that your holiday home is continually insured.

Our advice is to go to a specialist insurance provider; those companies who are knowledgeable about holiday homes offer policies specifically tailored to your needs.

We've got some examples here, together with a flavour of coverage you can expect.

Shield Total Insurance, for example, offers cover for loss, damage and theft as well as fire, lightning, subsidence, and even landslip. Fixed exterior storage boxes, balconies, steps and skirting are also covered, as is loss or damage from flooding, trees, fire and storm.

Among other specialist companies is Leisuredays, whose cover includes a new-for-old option. Adrian Flux also offers new-for-old cover on 'newer holiday homes'. Towergate Insurance's cover incudes new-for-old on holiday homes up to 20 years old and you can choose to include 'homecare emergency' as an additional product with your policy. Paul Baker Insurance Services is among other well-known specialists in the field of holiday home insurance, offering flexible insurance policies for a wide range of values. Coast Insurance includes cover for a wide variety of problems that may occur while you are staying in the holiday home or during periods it is left empty.

Shop around, just as you would for home insurance, and find a policy that best suits your needs.

12 | Buying Your First Holiday Home 2020

Renting out your holiday home

Some parks forbid you to rent out your holiday home. Others positively encourage it. Renting out makes it possible for you to recoup some of the investment in your holiday home, or even buy one purely for investment.

Some parks have very specific schemes for this. One example is Ladram Bay Holiday Park on the south Devon coast, which has a sublet scheme that includes everything from collecting payment to cleaning your holiday home, and also offers a guaranteed income whether or not the park fills the designated letting dates. Another example is Aria Resorts, which has a specific Aria Investments scheme. Parkdean Resorts is also an example of a parks group which has a lettings scheme.

> "Some parks have specific schemes that enable you to rent out your holiday home"

Age of holiday homes

Parks vary in the number of years you are allowed to keep a holiday home on a park. Many parks allow you to keep your holiday home for 20 years; others more, with the proviso that you keep it in top condition. A few, though, insist that you replace it after 10 years; some 15. Very clearly, the idea of all holiday homes on a park being reasonably new is so that the park always looks pristine.

The licence agreement to occupy a pitch states the specific period of time that your holiday home can be kept on the park.

Finance

With a very few exceptions, you can't get a conventional mortgage to fund a holiday home purchase – but you can get finance. In many cases, a park can arrange finance, or you could go to your own bank, or shop around, of course.

The Holgates group of seven parks in Cumbria and Lancashire, for example, offers specialist holiday home funding plans, backed by Black Horse which specialises in providing finance for holiday homes. You will be able to choose monthly repayments that you are comfortable with, generally up to seven years.

Among other examples of parks that offer finance schemes is Parkdean Resorts, which works with Black Horse and Barclays. And Away Resorts is a licensed credit broker and can put you in touch with specialist lenders in this field, among them Black Horse.

Manufacturer, Willerby, has a list of parks and dealers which participate in its finance scheme – go to willerby.com/finance through Hitachi Capital (UK).

ADVICE
The home

A 'single' unit – a Swift Bordeaux, 12 feet wide

Obvious start points in choosing a holiday home are your budget and the number of people who will be using the home. Price relates to size of the home, of course – so-called 'double' units are much wider than 'single' units, which are 12-14 feet wide. Price also relates to the level of luxury, as you'd expect.

So, a first factor to consider in picking a holiday home is the number of bedrooms. Go for a three-bedroom home if you are likely to have plenty of family members or friends joining you on a regular basis. Some holiday homes have sofa beds in the lounge, so that you can accommodate extra people on an occasional basis.

The next factor to consider is layout. The majority of holiday homes have open-plan layouts. Some, though, are more open plan than others. In some,

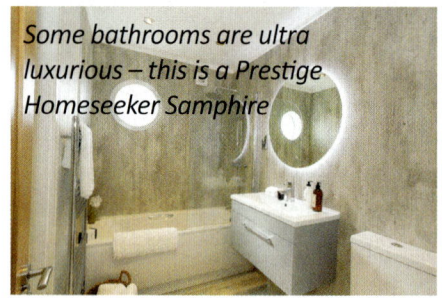

Some bathrooms are ultra luxurious – this is a Prestige Homeseeker Samphire

the kitchen is almost a separate entity yet integrates with the living space, so that the person cooking can still be involved in conversations.

Consider whether you want a breakfast bar; many high-end holiday homes have this feature – and it's a focal point of coffee conviviality.

Some holiday homes have just a toilet and washbasin en suite to the main bedroom; others have a shower, too. All have a main bathroom, which may have a bath with over-bath shower or a shower cubicle. These are points to consider as to what suits your family.

Also consider the amount of storage space. The longer you are planning to spend in your holiday home, the more storage space you will need. Look at the widths of wardrobes and the number of drawers. Some larger, luxurious homes have walk-in wardrobe-dressing rooms.

There is so much choice in layout that it's quite easy to find something that suits your requirements.

Once you get a clear idea of what layout will suit you, it's time to consider four-legged members of the family!

Dogs

Dogs are a major reason why people buy holiday homes. Anyone who has ever tried to rent a cottage or any other form of holiday home will know that finding pet-friendly accommodation is not easy. So, with your own holiday home, that problem goes away.

Dogs, though, do need a bit of thought when it comes to choosing the right layout. If you can avoid a layout in which muddy paws can get to a carpeted area before they've been cleaned, that will avoid a lot of stress.

Think about the flooring. Laminate is easily cleanable – and some holiday homes have that as standard, with lounge carpet as an option.

Some manufacturers cater in very specific ways for dogs. A very few homes have dog showers; that's the pinnacle of pet practicality!

One manufacturer caters in a very specific way for four-legged friends. Willerby's Simply Pawsome Pack is a range of specially designed equipment to make holidaying with dogs easy.

The option pack offers an outdoor

A dog shower in a Wessex Allure

tap, so that you can wash off the mud from your pooch's paws before they come inside; a retractable or rigid dog gate (pictured) to keep dogs out of the lounge, and a stable door (pictured) so that you can open the top half of the door to let some air in and know that the dogs can't get outside.

PARK & HOLIDAY HOME inspiration

ON YOUR iPAD

For further advice and information, don't miss *Park & Holiday Home Inspiration*. The best guide to finding and buying your perfect park or holiday home.

NOW PUBLISHED 6 TIMES A YEAR!

Enjoy all this:
- Read it on the go, wherever you may be!
- Save £££'s on print prices
- Get your issue before the printed version
- Environmentally friendly and much more!

Get your first digital issue for just **99p.** Then pay only **£1.99** an issue

pocketmags.com/park-and-holiday-home-inspiration-magazine

WILLERBY

HOMES FOR ALL TASTES AND WALLETS

Four holiday homes from the Willerby collection, all with very different styling – three models priced with affordability in mind and one with rather more luxury…

Willerby, the UK's largest holiday home manufacturer, offers a range of 14 holiday homes and four lodges, plus bespoke options.

We've reviewed four of Willerby's homes, in a variety of price brackets. These serve to illustrate that there's a Willerby holiday home for every taste and budget…

Ashurst

If you're looking for a bright, modern holiday home, the Ashurst deserves a place on your shortlist. It's one

Words **Val Chapman**

Ashurst

Ashurst

16 | Buying Your First Holiday Home 2020

Kelston

Kelston

A grade up from the Ashurst, the Kelston is two feet wider. It's available in four layout options, 36ft or 38ft long, both with two or three bedrooms.

The lounge seating is U-shaped, facing a unit which houses the log-effect fire. Distinctly different from the Ashurst in layout, the Kelston's dining table is within the kitchen; the hub of family life, one might say.

This home comes with a fridge-freezer as standard. Options include a gas central heating system, microwave, extractor fan and either a washer-dryer or a dishwasher.

The Kelston excels on storage space, with a walk-around wardrobe suite. The two-bedroom versions have king-sized beds in the main bedroom. You can opt for a double bed instead of twin beds in the second bedroom. And, as with the Ashurst, you can go for an upgraded mattress and a lift-up storage bed.

of Willerby's lowest-priced homes, yet it doesn't look or feel 'budget' category; just great value!

The Ashurst is a compact holiday home. It's one of just two 10ft-wide holiday homes from Willerby. It's available in three lengths, 28ft, 32ft and 35ft with two bedrooms, plus 35ft with three bedrooms.

The beauty of Willerby's affordable range is that buyers have options. As standard, the Ashurst has a gas-powered water heater and an electric fire in the lounge. If you plan to use your holiday home in the colder months, you can upgrade to the optional central heating system with condensing combi boiler.

Both the lounge and dining seating in the Ashurst are L-shaped; the result is plenty of floor space in the centre of the living area. The free-standing table is a cleverly designed triangular shape, again to preserve plenty of floor space. Two circular stools are there to be positioned wherever you need them.

Kitchen equipment is an oven-grill and hob. Optional extras include a fridge-freezer, a slimline dishwasher, a microwave and an extractor fan. So you can buy what you need and you're not paying for equipment that you'd rather not have.

Two showgrounds to browse

Willerby has two showgrounds where you can browse through many of the homes at your leisure. One is close to the factory in Hull (HU9 5WA); the other is in Scotland, half an hour from Edinburgh, at Livingston, West Lothian (EH52 6PA).
Make an appointment before you go; a member of the team will meet you and give you all of the information you need.

WILLERBY

Skye

Up another grade from the Kelston is the Skye. It's the same width as the Kelston, at 12 feet. This model has five layout options, three of them with three bedrooms, and varying in length between 28ft and 38ft.

If you're looking for a holiday home with a spacious lounge-dining area, the Skye is one to consider. The L-shaped lounge joins with the dining area, giving you lots of options as to how to use the space. Kick back and relax anywhere on the seating area's vast space, or move the freestanding table around to dine where it suits you – in front of your TV or well away from the main lounge area – the choice is yours.

The Skye has an open-plan layout but with an unusual twist; an angled part-wall (the place for your TV, with shelving above) creates a divider from the kitchen. On the other side of the divider, the microwave sits at an angle, with cabinets below it, giving the kitchen an interesting dimension.

A fridge freezer, microwave and extractor fan are standard. A washer-dryer or a dishwasher are options.

You can also opt for French doors at the front of the unit, a Bluetooth MP3 system and a gas central heating system.

18 | Buying Your First Holiday Home 2020

Waverley

The Waverley represents a big step up from the Skye and is one of Willerby's premium holiday homes. Central heating comes as standard. The kitchen has an island unit breakfast bar. A five-burner hob is standard. And there's a recess opposite the entrance, with a seat with shoe rack.

Residential specification (which involves extra insulation as well as other benefits) is an option, so you can order your Waverley designed for use at any time of the year; that's ideal if you are considering siting it on a park that is open all year.

The Waverley is a step up in size, too; it's 14 feet wide and 42ft long. It's available in two layouts, one with two bedrooms, one with three.

The kitchen is stunning in style, with a breakfast bar on one side of the island unit, which is illuminated by two stunning copper and black lights.

Lighting in the main bedroom is impressive, too (as our inset picture shows) – and this bedroom has a king-size bed with a lift up storage area, plus a window seat!

Another notable feature is that the twin beds are three feet wide. The Waverley is one to consider if you aspire to luxury alongside practicality.

Contact
Willerby
Hull Showground, Great Field Lane, Marfleet Lane, Hull, East Yorkshire HU9 5WA
01482 717599
willerby.com

WILLERBY OWNERS' CLUB

BEE A MEMBER!

Owners of Willerby holiday homes are invited to become members of a club which offers discounts, competitions, invitations and free tickets

Owning a Willerby holiday home gets you more than a leisure lifestyle. It entitles you to become a member of a club.

The Willerby Owners' Club is free to join and is open to buyers of pre-owned Willerby holiday homes as well as new ones. It's also open to owners of BK Bluebird holiday homes, because this manufacturer is a part of the Willerby empire.

The Willerby Owners' Club was launched just a year ago and already has 5,000 members.

Members get:

● **WELCOME PACK**

A free welcome pack of goodies including limited-edition mugs – and a packet of wildflower seeds. That's to encourage you to plant flowers that will attract bees. It's all part of Willerby's Bumblebee Conservation Trust work.

Willerby launched the campaign dedicated to bumblebee conservation in 2017, to celebrate the 70th year since the company's foundation.

The link between bees and Willerby goes back more than 70 years, though. Walter Allen, founder of Willerby, had a business building beehives in the post-war years – before he saw a gap in the embryonic holiday market, and started building touring caravans. The company progressed quickly to become the UK's largest maker of holiday homes and now also has a range of residential homes plus new bespoke lodges in its vast portfolio.

● **DISCOUNTS**
Members are offered discounts on a range of outdoor furniture, ideal to enhance holiday home decking areas.

They also get special offers and free tickets to shows including the Caravan, Motorhome and Holiday Home Expo at the Yorkshire Event Centre in Harrogate, which takes place 11-13 September.

● **COMPETITIONS**
A range of competitions take place; typically, there are exotic hampers to be won, plus luxury spa breaks!

● **NEWSLETTERS**
Members also receive regular newsletters to keep up with the latest developments from this energetic manufacturer.

● **INVITATIONS**
Members are invited to join focus groups dedicated to development of the company's holiday homes; this is an exciting chance to influence the Willerby holiday homes of the future.

There are also invitations to preview events at Willerby's showground close to the factory in Hull, and opportunities to speak with the designers of the holiday homes, to get to know more about how a Willerby holiday home is created.

Order a brochure today!
Call **0345 257 0400**
email **info@wessexparkhomes.co.uk**
or visit **wessexparkhomes.co.uk**

THE CLASSIC

Luxury Lodge

Unique lodges and park homes with a 50 year heritage, built upon industry leading design, quality and excellent customer service.

Built to BS 3632 residential standard | 10-year GoldShield structural warranty
Superior build quality | Bespoke design solutions | Industry leading customer care

WESSEX
UNIQUE LODGES & PARK HOMES

T: 0345 257 0400   **E:** sales@wessexparkhomes.co.uk   **W:** wessexparkhomes.co.uk

WESSEX UNIQUE LODGES & PARK HOMES, PLESZKO HOUSE, LONDON ROAD, BRANDON, SUFFOLK IP27 ONE

WESSEX UNIQUE LODGES AND PARK HOMES

COUNTRY-STYLE LUXURY

Three country-style luxury lodges: one with a snug, a pantry and a shower for dogs, one with a four-poster bed – and one with handcrafted wicker dining chairs

Wessex Allure

With a split-level roofline and two sets of bifold doors, the Allure, one of eight luxury lodges in the Wessex range, is a striking holiday home even before you step inside. Then, you realise that this is an extraordinary lodge. And it's not only designed for family conviviality, it's specifically designed with dogs in mind.

There's a dog shower by the door, so that you can eliminate any muddy paw problems before your 'best friend' makes an escape towards the living space. Even if that happens, the designers have thought of that too – the flooring is laminate and so it's easily washable. If you'd rather not have a dog shower, you can have a utility room instead, at no extra cost.

Another feature of the Allure that makes it special is that it has a snug – a cosy room which sits to one side of the lounge, complete with a love seat and a suite of larch shelves – a perfect place in which to retreat with a book. This room can have many functions. It can be a morning coffee room or a music room; a place in which to retreat from the lounge. And if your family includes school-age people, the snug is an ideal homework room, meaning that holidays and breaks can have just the same

WESSEX UNIQUE LODGES AND PARK HOMES

routine, when needed, as home.

Practicality abounds in the Allure – and it starts the moment you walk through the door, with coathooks, shelving, somewhere to perch to lace and unlace boots – and wicker basket drawers in which to tidy away your footwear. Those wicker drawers give a first clue to the country character of the Allure. The same delightful wicker styling appears in the breakfast bar, the sideboard and seating-storage units in the snug. We love it! We also love the amazing glass box pendant triple light above the country-style extending dining table. The Allure is alluring in so many ways!

That includes the kitchen, where there is another surprising feature – a walk-in pantry. As you'd expect, there is a full array of integrated appliances and an abundance of cabinet space.

The country feel continues in the bedrooms. The main bedroom has waxed oak furniture and a velvet-upholstered chair alongside full-height windows; perfect for morning coffee!

The Allure is an amazing lodge, with many elements that offer you flexibility and choice – dog shower or utility room, for example – and there's an alternative specification, too. The Allure Deluxe has a Corian Burled Beach worktop; the worktop in the standard Allure is laminate. There's an exterior difference, too; the Deluxe version is clad in larch, whereas the standard Allure has CanExel cladding. Whatever you choose, the Allure guarantees you country-style luxury mixed with practicality.

The Allure Deluxe and Allure come in two standard sizes, 50ft, with three bedrooms, and 45ft, with two bedrooms. Both are 20ft wide. And all of the homes in the range can be bespoke tailored to suit individual taste and requirements.

Spinney

The Spinney takes country style a step further than the Allure, with a distinctly woodland vibe. This is created by a distressed oak mantelpiece, a feature wall with an electric stove set into a tiled hearth, plus wallpaper in a stacked log style. And there's more. The Spinney has a four-poster bed!

The first time we reviewed the Spinney, shortly after it was unveiled, we were bowled over by what we described as 'the most stunning table we've yet seen in a lodge'. It's a huge, rustic, single plank-effect table with matching benches. Our review continued: 'This awesome dining suite seems to encapsulate the Spinney's country, natural feel.' We were also impressed by the kitchen position, secluded from the lounge-dining area and with a side door leading into it.

The stunning elements of this lodge continue in the en suite where there's a freestanding bath and a separate shower with overhead soaker. The Spinney has the word 'luxury' running right through it. There's delightful oak furniture in the twin room, heated towel rails in both the en suite and shower room and, in the family shower room, a shower fitted with a valve that ensures there is no delay in maintaining the water temperature when switching between the fixed shower head and hand-held rose.

The Spinney is available in five standard sizes. All are 20ft or 22ft wide. Four have two bedrooms; these are 40ft, 45ft and 50ft versions, plus 45ft and 50ft versions which have a walk-through wet-room with a bath. There's also a 50ft three-bedroom version.

WESSEX UNIQUE LODGES AND PARK HOMES

Classic

Like the Spinney and Allure, the Classic has a country style – but this time it's more subtle, and with a neutral palette.

The living area has a light and airy feel, created by triangular windows above the French doors and triple panel full height window. The ceiling is vaulted and white-panelled, enhancing the feeling of space.

The lounge seating is sumptuous – two big settees upholstered in a 'stone' shade fabric, plus a cosy little chair, with a detailed diamond pattern in the weave. Lots of cushions, in a variety of stone and neutral shades, ensure you can get cosy.

Amid the neutral shades that characterise the Classic, there's a stunning style statement. The extending dining table is teamed with handcrafted wicker chairs; their texture and style epitomise the country character of the Classic. And their high back and shape makes them extremely comfortable.

Kitchen styling is appealingly plain and modern, with gloss cream cabinet doors, all with soft-close mechanisms.

The country theme continues in the bedrooms, with shaker-style white furniture and a continuation of the soft, neutral colour palette.

Five standard sizes are available. All are 20ft wide. The 36ft, 38ft, 40ft and 45ft versions have two bedrooms; there is also a 42ft version with three bedrooms. Two of the layouts have utility rooms; these are the 40ft and 45ft units

⟨ Contact ⟩
Wessex Unique Lodges & Park Homes
Pleszko House, London Road, Brandon, Suffolk IP27 0NE
0345 257 0400
wessexparkhomes.co.uk

Order a brochure today!

Call
01842 810 673

email
sales@omar.co.uk

or visit
www.omar.co.uk

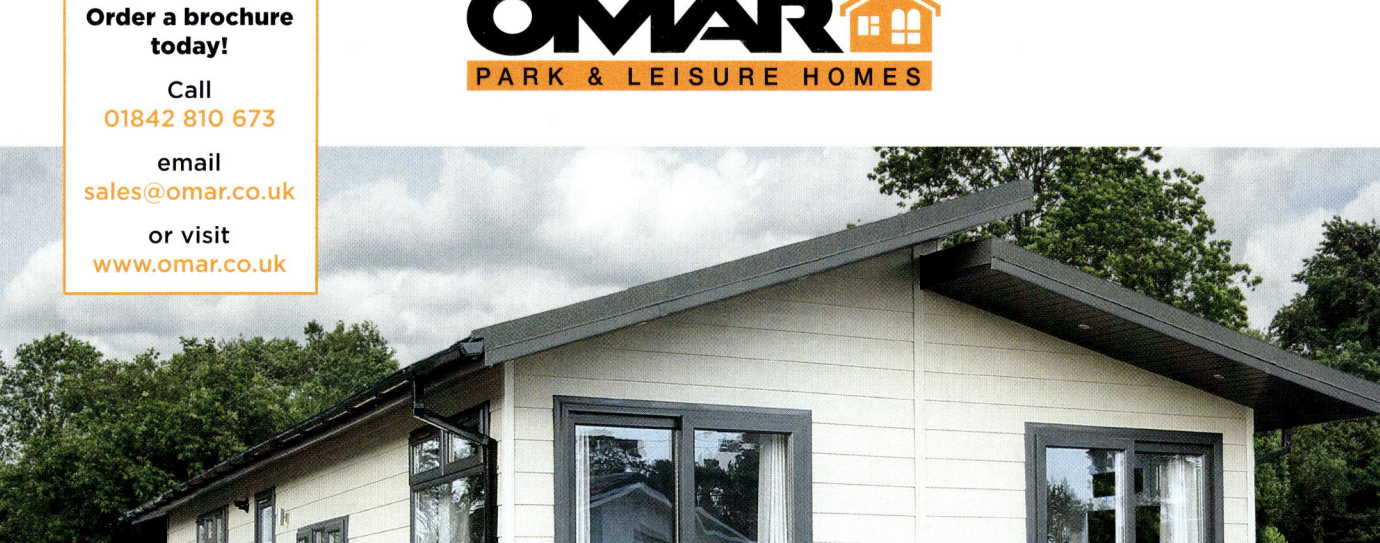

ALDERNEY LUXURY LODGE

A contemporary and light **luxury lodge** with distinctive design features, providing holiday practicality in Omar style luxury!

- Built to BS 3632 residential standard and protected by a 10-year GoldShield structural warranty
- Split, pitched, Shingle profile tiled roof with extended front soffit (roof tiles guaranteed for 40 years)
- CanExel, Ced'R-Vue, 9" lap cladding (other colours and claddings available)
- Two sets of patio doors, large full height picture windows and a skylight to the lounge
- Two double bedrooms and a third single bedroom/study (on selected floor plans)
- White panelled ceilings throughout

Omar Park & Leisure Homes, Head Office & Show Centre, Pleszko House, London Road, Brandon, Suffolk IP27 0NE

www.omar.co.uk | 01842 810 673 | sales@omar.co.uk

OMAR PARK & LEISURE HOMES

Words **Val Chapman**

FOR ALL TASTES

Three holiday homes from Omar's range of lodges – this manufacturer offers something to suit all budgets and tastes

Atrium Monopitch

An enormous central lounge with a huge expanse of windows – and bedrooms at opposite ends, the Atrium Monopitch makes a big statement in the lodge world. This is a family lodge for buyers looking at the upper end of the luxury spectrum.

Because it has bedrooms at each end, its appeal is ultra-flexible. It's great for families, and equally great

if you have guests; that's because the two bedrooms are in separate areas of the lodge. Both have doors to lead out onto your decking.

This lodge's name derives from the slope of its roof – and from the large, glazed central doors which open into the vast open-plan kitchen-lounge-dining space. This is leisure lounge luxury and style taken to top level, with a large, L-shaped sofa and a sumptuously comfortable armchair facing the big window area and a hand-crafted mango wood coffee table in the centre of the lounge.

Notable, also, is the farmhouse-style dining table with benches, and the kitchen that provides plenty of cooking space. It's equipped with a dishwasher, washing machine, a five-burner hob – and even a wine cooler.

The Atrium Monopitch's look is one of ultra-modernity with a hint of country styling. The bold turquoise accent colour – which appears in cushions, blinds, the upholstery of the armchair and 10 tiles in the kitchen – injects a sunny day, blue sky appeal to the décor.

The Atrium Monopitch that we review here is the 45ft by 20ft layout. Other standard sizes available are a 50ft by 20ft version, with three bedrooms, and a 40ft by 20ft version with two bedrooms.

OMAR PARK & LEISURE HOMES

Alderney

One of Omar's mid-range lodges, the Alderney has styling with just a suggestion of coast meets country, with coffee tables and the dining table that mix driftwood with shaker style.

It has a split-level roofline which creates a stylish and distinctive look. Like the Atrium Monopitch, the Alderney is very much a family lodge.

Named after the third-2largest Channel island, the Alderney is open plan, light and airy, with settees facing each other across the lounge and plenty of space in the centre.

The six-seater dining suite is positioned by one of the five floor-to-ceiling windows.

The kitchen is galley style. A five-burner hob is set into the unit which divides the kitchen from the dining area. The fridge-freezer and oven face each other, out of the way at the end of the kitchen; a very practical layout.

Three cupboards are in the hallway, adjacent to a door which leads into the dining area; these are brilliant for hiding away all manner of holiday kit. From here, the corridor leads to a bathroom with over-bath shower, and three bedrooms. One has a single bed and a desk so that it can double as a study, making it ideal for school holiday work arrangements; another has twin beds. All three bedrooms have good storage capacity.

This is a lodge to consider if you need family flexibility – somewhere quiet for homework, just as at home – plus plenty of space for family conviviality. We love this lodge!

The unit we review here is the 45ft by 20ft, three-bedroom version. The Alderney is available in six standard sizes, all 20ft wide, ranging in length from 36ft to 50ft. Two of the versions have three bedrooms.

30 | Buying Your First Holiday Home 2020

Southwold

If you're looking for a smaller, single lodge, the Southwold is one to consider. Omar designed it to offer a luxurious yet affordable introduction to the holiday lodge lifestyle. The Southwold – named after the character seaside town in Suffolk – is a smaller lodge (in a choice of 14ft or 15ft wide); it's known as a 'single unit', compared to the Atrium Monopitch and Alderney, which are double units. Yet, like all of Omar's lodges, it's built to residential standards, which means it's designed to be used at any time of the year.

Double doors lead from the fully glazed front of the Southwold into the lounge, where soft blues and greys create a seashore look that evokes a holiday atmosphere. The fireplace houses an amazing fire feature: wave-pounded rocks in a white oval bowl with flickering flames.

Two armchairs and a settee provide the comfort; a shaker-style coffee table with storage box provides the practicality. So, too, does the size of the circular dining table, which extends to an oval shape, to seat six. The lounge feels quite separate from the kitchen-dining area, which sit opposite one another. The kitchen has ample storage space. Appliances include a washing machine and dishwasher.

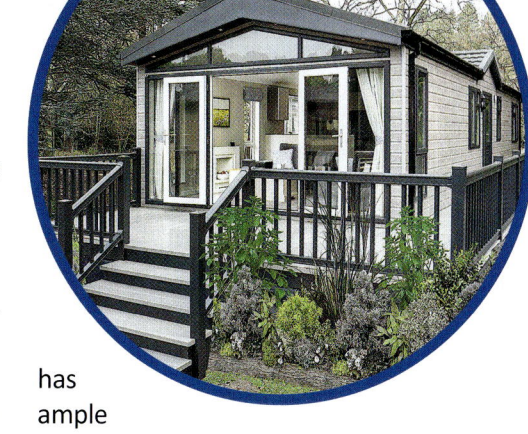

Beautiful wood-grain-effect tiles and mirrored cabinets are in both the en suite and family shower room.

When choosing your Southwold, there's another lodge in Omar's range to look at. It's the Westfield – because the décor is interchangeable between the two. So, if you prefer the fawns and creams in the Westfield, you can opt for that scheme in the Southwold.

The Southwold is available in six standard sizes. These range from 40ft by 14ft to 45ft by 15ft. All have two bedrooms.

Contact
Omar Park & Leisure Homes
Pleszko House, London Road,
Brandon, Suffolk IP27 0NE
01842 810673
omar.co.uk

PATHFINDER HOMES

EXCEPTIONAL OPPORTUNITIES!

Two exclusive parks are being developed in the southwest – one in Cornwall and one in Devon, both in stunning elevated locations

If you fancy a leisure lodge in a very special location, on the edge of spectacular moorland, with amazing views, yet also within easy distance of a great many places of interest, read on, for there are two developments taking place in the southwest, both featuring lodges by specialist manufacturer, Pathfinder Homes. And both offer exceptional holiday home purchase opportunities.

One is taking shape on the edge of Bodmin Moor in Cornwall, the other in Devon...

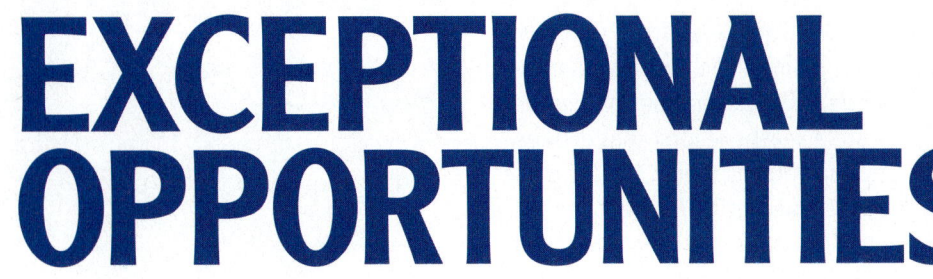

Springfield Retreat

Eight miles west of Exeter lies a holiday lodge park where an exciting new development is taking place. The park is on the fringe of the Dartmoor National Park, close to the A30 that takes you into Cornwall, so it's ideally placed for exploring both Devon and Cornwall.

The park will be home to luxury lodges, made by Devon manufacturer, Pathfinder, sited on elevated pitches with stunning views – and buyers will have the opportunity to have hot tubs! Eight lodges, designed

Words **Val Chapman**

Images Lucy Brown

specifically for the park, will form the first phase of the development, together with a new name for the park – Springfield Retreat.

This park has, until now, been called Springfield Holiday Park. Now, it not only gets a new name, but also the start of a transformation to become a luxury leisure retreat. The first eight lodges will be sited in a gated area.

You can buy a lodge as your leisure retreat, or as a buy-to-let investment. And Springfield Retreat will offer both part-exchange and finance options.

And the lodges? They have a name that is of great significance in the region where the park sits: The Tor.

Tor is a Celtic word for large rock outcrop, but in Devon and Cornwall the term is used also to mean hill. Dartmoor has many tors, among them Fur Tor, rated as the most remote tor on Dartmoor and a challenge for walkers; Great Staple Tor; Great Links Tor; Leather Tor; Sharp Tor; Black Tor... the list goes on.

And now, these new Tor lodges give a totally new meaning to the ancient word.

The Tor lodge is a really special creation, available in both single and twin versions. The design combines a feeling of space and comfort along with plenty of storage and practicality. It has a basic yet creative interior scheme; you can choose your Tor as standard or put your own stamp on it. The essence of The Tor is that it includes all of the necessities of lodge living at an affordable price.

Warm whites and pastel greens create a relaxed environment in the lounge-dining area and the kitchen is smart white.

The main bedroom has an en suite and walk-in wardrobe. The second bedroom has single beds, a built-in wardrobe and a full-length window.

PATHFINDER HOMES

Higher Charaton Park

Higher Charaton is a very special place for a number of reasons. That's not just about its stunning location in the gorgeous countryside of Cornwall, but because here, you not only buy the lodge but the land on which it sits, too. This will be the only park in the southwest offering lodges for sale on a freehold basis, so no ground rent will be payable. Another unique aspect of this park is that all of the lodges can be designed to be accessible to disabled people. Plus, there will be only nine lodges on this park, so that's yet another aspect of exclusivity!

And there's more... The lodges being built for Higher Charaton Park will be based on Pathfinder's Retreat lodge, with upgrades – and buyers will have the opportunity to design their own homes!

The park is being established on the edge of the village of Pensilva, five miles from Liskeard and with views that stretch far over Dartmoor, from the serene Bodmin moorland to the valleys along the River Tamar.

Close to the park is a farm shop, a pub and a community centre with a gym. Liskeard has restaurants, pubs and supermarkets and so does Callington, six miles away. The farm

34 | Buying Your First Holiday Home 2020

It's time, to make time...

STUNNING HOLIDAY HOMES FOR SALE

THIS PARK OFFERS A UNIQUE
FREEHOLD OPPORTUNITY
NO SITE FEES TO PAY... EVER!

Nestled in the beautiful Cornish countryside, Higher Charaton Park is perfectly placed for your holiday base.

With views that stretch far and wide over Dartmoor, from the serene views atop Bodmin to the luscious valleys along the River Tamar. Everything you need is a stone's throw from the park, including a local farm shop, public house and community hall. All just a short drive from neighbouring cities & local attractions.

- Zero site fees... forever
- Design your own home
- Accessible plots available
- 12 Month holiday license
- Beautiful Cornwall location
- Buy-to-let options
- Finance Available*

*Subject to availability, acceptance and valuation

Call us today
01626 833 799

info@paladinparkhomes.co.uk

LUXURIOUS, HIGH QUALITY, **ALL YOURS!**

Offering you the opportunity to design your very own home, lucky enough to have the UK's leading luxury lodge Manufacturer close by; Pathfinder Homes will carefully design and craft each and every home, with you in mind. You can even visit their factory and choose your own layout, furniture and finishing!

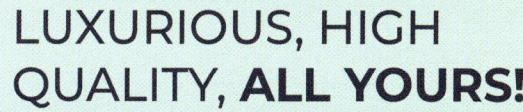

www.highercharaton.co.uk
Higher Charaton Park, Pensilva, Liskeard PL14 5RW
A Pathfinder Homes Exclusive Park. A Paladin Park Homes Development

Higher Charaton PARK

Show home now open

UPCOMING OPEN DAYS
Come and explore our fabulous Show home on park

| March 14th | April 25th | May 30th | June 27th |

DISCOVER MORE ABOUT THIS UNIQUE FREEHOLD OPPORTUNITY

PATHFINDER HOMES

THE SAME BUT DIFFERENT

- Smart Lighting
- Keyless Locks
- Smart Heating
- CCTV
- Electric Car Charger

Imagine after a lengthy day exploring the local landscape, going back to a warm, safe, well-lit home – you don't even have to fumble around looking for yours keys!

Leading in the industry, our Smart Homes offer peace-of-mind for the whole family, from checking that the four legged family member is safe, to adjusting the heating before you get through the door.

01626 833 799

www.pathfinderhomes.co.uk

INNOVATION · INSPIRATION · IMAGINATION

You're invited! Open days have been announced at Higher Charaton Park. These will take place on 14 March, 25 April, 30 May and 27 June.

shop sells artisan breads, Cornish gins, honey and ales and even Cornish-made chocolate.

And further afield? You'll never be short of things to do in this region. There are the famous attractions of the Eden Project and Lost Gardens of Heligan, plus the pretty ports of Looe, Polperro, Fowey and Mevagissey. The beaches and bays of the spectacular north coast are not far away. Cornwall's cathedral city, Truro, is only an hour away. And, just over the Devon border, 20 miles from the park, is the waterfront city of Plymouth, with theatres, historical interest and a great many eating opportunities.

The lodges will be built to residential standard, ensuring you're comfortable even in the colder months. The park has a 12-month holiday licence.

A hot tub and decking and a private landscaped courtyard are part of the Higher Charaton Park experience.

Contact
Pathfinder Homes
Armada House, Cavalier Rd,
Heathfield Industrial Estate,
Newton Abbot TQ12 6FJ
pathfinderhomes.co.uk
01626 833799

TINGDENE HOMES

AMAZING DESIGNS!

A roof terrace, a centre lounge, Scandinavian style, country or woodland theme, intriguing industrial chic... Tingdene holiday homes have spectacular features and styles. We review five of them here

Tingdene Homes offers a range of 12 holiday lodges, all stunning in their own ways – but one is more stunning than the others... That's the Quantum.

Quantum

Unveiled last summer, the Quantum was the undoubted star of the park and holiday home shows, towering above surrounding homes and grabbing the limelight. The reason? The huge Quantum has a roof terrace spanning the entire length and breadth of the lodge.

This fabulous terrace, designed for entertaining, is bordered by glass panels, so you feel that it's totally open, yet there is shelter from the breeze. It incorporates a barbecue area and lots of space for sitting, chatting and enjoying the very best of a sophisticated holiday home lifestyle. Plus, there's space for a hot tub. If you aspire to the ultimate in holiday lodge lifestyle, the Quantum is surely one to consider.

Tingdene calls the Quantum a revolution in luxury lodge living. This is a 52ft by 22ft lodge, with a bedroom at each end – one a double, one a twin.

Décor is nothing short of fantastic; an amalgam of cutting-edge designs

36 | Buying Your First Holiday Home 2020

Harrington

If you're drawn to Scandinavian-inspired style, you'll love the open-plan layout Harrington. Shades of taupe and natural linen are teamed with pale grey to create an ultra-calm look. This lodge is also characterised by its huge lounge windows; two of them are opening doors. You'd really feel in touch with the outdoors in this room.

The design of this 40ft by 20ft lodge is infused with Scandinavian style elements in all areas – simple lines, louvre wall insets, bright white kitchen units.

It has some stunning furniture designs, too, including two small, quirky rocking chairs in the lounge and a feature wall of textured grey inset into a bold white frame. Spotlights focus down to a white shelved area that stretches the entire length of the lounge.

The Harrington's entrance hallway has a place for coats and shoes and a cushioned seat; no excuses for not taking off your shoes as you step inside!

An open-shelved divider sits between the hallway and the lounge, keeping the open-plan look while also creating a demarcation.

The kitchen is galley-style, in that it is arranged in a parallel configuration but it's much wider than classic galley kitchens, and with a full-height window at the head of the 'galley'. Over the breakfast bar are three filament-bulb, conical glass pendant lights; four upholstered bar chairs are up to the breakfast bar.

The dining area benefits from the big-window theme of the lounge; windows are on both sides of this area. The table is extendable to seat six; two extra chairs can be purchased.

Chrome pendant lights over the dining table and lounge look stunning.

including a kitchen wall clad in an amazing geometric wood veneer design in black and pale wood and, in the en suite to the guest bedroom, hexagonal-shaped tiles in dark blue, orange, black, yellow, grey and white.

The master bedroom suite's design is awesome, with an island wall separating the bedroom from the free-standing bath, enormous, open shower, the toilet in its own separate room, a copper radiator (yes, really!) and a walk-in wardrobe with a row of LEDs set into the rail!

The colossal Quantum makes a statement of breathtaking style; it's arguably the ultimate in holiday lodge elegance. Yet Tingdene's portfolio of homes for leisure and homes for living also contains lots of options for buyers looking for much more modest alternatives.

TINGDENE HOMES

Havana

The Havana is a classic lodge with elegant, modern looks and touches of industrial chic. And it's available in three layout options. You can go for one, two or three bedrooms, and can even have a utility room if you wish.

There's a one-bedroom version, 40ft by 16ft. There are two 42ft by 20ft options, one with two double rooms and one with a twin room. Whichever of these layouts you choose, both of the bedrooms have walk-in wardrobes and en suites. One of the 42ft by 20ft options has a dog shower in the utility room; this model is called Havana Pet Friendly!

The kitchen in all three layouts has ample wow factor, with slate grey worktops and offset, 'floating' warm-tone wooden shelving. The anthracite shade gloss-finished units offer plenty of storage space.

Appliances include a five-zone induction hob set into the breakfast bar unit plus oven, fridge-freezer, dishwasher and wine cooler.

We love the bar stools that have a rustic industrial look. They are a combination of black wrought iron and reclaimed-style wood.

The dining area has four brown leather chairs with black metal finishings. The leather has a traditional distressed look, adding to the industrial style theme.

Rockingham

The Rockingham gives you three layout options, too – this time in a very different style. It's an exceptionally spacious lodge, with a spectacular split roofline, enormous windows to the open-plan living area and three large porthole mirrors to make a style statement.

The lounge-dining-kitchen area is immense, spanning the divide between the two sections of the lodge – one with a flat roof, the other with an angled roof.

The section of the lodge which has an angled roof is clad in grey, whereas the flat-roofed section alongside it is finished in contrasting cedar-effect; utterly stunning!

The lounge

38 | Buying Your First Holiday Home 2020

has an intriguing design, with two seating areas. At the front, two small armchairs are positioned by the window, to take advantage of sun warming through the glass – and of the view. The main lounge area, with two settees facing one another, has an innovative-design, huge coffee table, composed of three squares, set at differing angles.

Apricot and pink are the accent colours of the Rockingham. Combined with cool greys and fawns, it looks delightful. Lounge cushions are in a variety of textures, ranging from light-reflecting sheen to velvet.

The Rockingham is available in two and three-bedroomed layouts and in sizes ranging from 40ft by 20ft to 50ft by 20ft. The 50ft by 20ft Rockingham has a double bedroom plus two twin-bed rooms.

Savannah

The Savannah offers four layout choices – and two décor themes. You can have a Savannah with either coastal or woodland vibes. Styling is rather like the Havana, so if you like this model, take a close look, also, at the Havana.

Perhaps most important among the options is that you can have a Savannah with bedrooms at each end and the lounge and dining-kitchen in the centre. That's an ideal layout for two generations, especially as both bedrooms have en suites.

Size options are 40ft by 12ft for the centre-lounge model, and 38ft or 42ft by 13ft for the options which have the lounge at the front of the layout.

There are very few centre-lounge holiday homes on the market, which is why we so love this option in the Savannah range. It has an ingenious layout, with a full-height part wall, forming the demarcation line between the kitchen and the lounge.

On the lounge side, the part wall's purpose is a media wall, with sockets for a television. On the kitchen side, the wall has another function – it has a deep, natural walnut panel with three recessed shelves; quite stunning. Natural walnut is a theme that runs throughout the kitchen, with 'floating' shelves, like those in the Havana, within the breakfast bar unit.

The four-burner hob is set into the breakfast bar unit, with an oval extractor fan above it. The oven is directly below it, keeping the cooking equipment conveniently in one area. The fridge-freezer and dishwasher are contained within the units.

The pale blue colour of the kitchen surfaces carries through to the lounge, where a single armchair is upholstered in this shade. The L-shaped sofa is plain, pale grey. The whole look is smartly retro.

Contact

Tingdene Homes
Bradfield Road, Finedon Road Industrial Estate, Wellingborough, Northamptonshire NN8 4HB
01933 230130
tingdene.co.uk

■ Difference #39

REDEFINING LODGE LIVING

Everything we do is, and always has been, designed around you. That's why you'll feel 50 years of passion, craftsmanship and knowledge in every one of our British-built luxury lodges. And with Tingdene, you can trust that we'll share every bit of our experience to ensure your move runs smoothly. From the moment you select your specification to the day you move in.

Experience the difference for yourself, take a tour of our lodges and homes at our indoor showroom in Wellingborough – we can't wait to welcome you.

T/50 Since 1969

Discover the difference

Park Homes + Holiday Lodges
tingdene.co.uk | 01933 230 130

Quality | Heritage | Passion | Innovation

Artistic impression. Actual exterior and interior lodge design may vary.

ADVICE

10 THINGS
to consider when buying a holiday home
Buying Your First Holiday Home's at-a-glance guide

1 HOW MUCH DO I NEED TO SPEND?
You can buy a pre-owned holiday home for around £20,000 or maybe even less. Or you can go for a super-luxury, architect-designed lodge for well over £500,000. In between, there's a vast choice. So there are holiday homes for every budget.
  Our tip: Set your budget depending on the amount of time you're are likely to use the holiday home. If you are going to spend every holiday and every weekend there, it's worth considering spending more than if you plan on using it only occasionally.

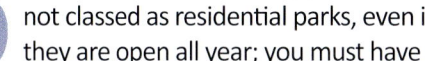

2 WHAT ON-GOING COSTS DO I NEED TO BUDGET FOR?
Budget for pitch fees, gas, electricity and insurance.

3 CAN I PART EXCHANGE?
Some parks take touring caravans and motorhomes in part-exchange for holiday homes. That can be a very attractive option, bearing in mind that it can be difficult to sell, privately, a touring caravan or motorhome of a high value – that's because most buyers, understandably, prefer to go to a dealer.
  Our advice, though, is to try to sell your touring caravan or motorhome privately; you may just get more for it than from a holiday park. It's worth a try!

4 DO I NEED TO INSURE MY HOLIDAY HOME?
Yes. All parks insist that you have an insurance policy in place and most will want to see it every year.

5 HOW LONG CAN I KEEP MY HOLIDAY HOME?
Licence agreements are in place on all holiday home parks. These vary from 10 to 15 years and considerably more.

6 CAN I LIVE IN MY HOLIDAY HOME?
No. this is because holiday parks are not classed as residential parks, even if they are open all year; you must have a permanent residential address elsewhere.

7 CAN I HIRE MY HOLIDAY HOME OUT?
Some parks permit this; others don't.

8 CAN I LOAN MY HOLIDAY HOME TO MY FRIENDS AND FAMILY?
Yes. But you can only hire a holiday home out for money on parks which permit this.

9 CAN I USE FINANCE TO PURCHASE A HOLIDAY HOME?
Yes; many parks have links with finance companies which specialise in holiday home purchase.

10 DO I NEED A TELEVISION LICENCE FOR MY HOLIDAY HOME?
If you have a television licence registered at your main address, you don't need another one for your holiday home.

OAKGROVE HOLIDAY LODGES

Words **Val Chapman**

SOPHISTICATED AND SPACIOUS

Stacked with luxury features including bathroom underfloor heating, a free-standing bath and granite worktops, the Tamarack is available with up to four bedrooms

Oakgrove's Tamarack Lodge has a large open-plan living area and lots of elements that combine to make it a high-quality, luxurious and sophisticated holiday retreat. These include a Velux rooflight in the kitchen, a free-standing bath, heated towel rails in both the main bathroom and en suite, underfloor heating in the bathrooms, and granite worktops.

The entrance is recessed and has a peaked roofline. You step into a semi-enclosed entrance hall with storage space – and then into the open-plan lounge, dining and kitchen area.

It's very much a family lodge – you can choose your Tamarack with up to four bedrooms. The focal point of the lounge is a contemporary real flame-effect fire. In the kitchen, the skylight ensures an abundance of daylight. There's a five-burner hob, a built-in oven and microwave, an integrated fridge-freezer, dishwasher and washer-dryer.

The main bedroom has a hidden en suite which you enter through slide-door wardrobes.

There are various sizes available to suite you or your park's requirements.

All of Oakgrove's lodges are constructed to the residential BS 3632 standard.

Design office in Bristol to visit

Buyers can visit Oakgrove's design office in Bristol, by appointment, where they can choose and design their lodge with the company's interiors team. On show is a range of designs and finishes from Oakgrove's suppliers, with over 100 soft furnishing fabrics to choose from, plus a range of tiles and flooring choices. The team can also advise on kitchen finishes and furniture to suit your taste.

Contact
Oakgrove Lodges
& Park Homes
Carrakeel Drive, Maydown,
Londonderry,
Northern Ireland BT47 6UQ
028 7186 1166
oakgrovelodges.co.uk

OAKGROVE
Lodges and Park Homes

www.oakgrovelodges.co.uk info@oakgrovelodges.co.uk
@OakgroveLodgesandParkHomes @oakgrove_lodgesandparkhomes

Create your holiday home with
Oakgrove Lodges and Park Homes
Where your dream holiday home becomes a reality!

FAMILY RUN PARK WITH ACCESS ONTO THE PURBECK HILLS & ONLY A MILE FROM THE JURASSIC COAST.

Ulwell HOLIDAY PARK

NEW HOLIDAY HOMES AVAILABLE FOR SALE FOR THE 2020 SEASON

SEE WEBSITE FOR DETAILS www.ulwellholidaypark.co.uk
01929 422 823 | enq@ulwellholidaypark.co.uk

Park is open March 1st - January 7th. Reception is open all year.

Opens 1st March

Insurance tailored around you and your Park Home

Whatever your pride and joy, you could save time and money by calling Adrian Flux when your insurance renewal is due. Our policies are tailored to your specific requirements which means **you won't find us on comparison websites**...

Competitive insurance for park home policies.
Call us today on 0800 085 5000 for a free, no obligation quote.

0800 085 5000
adrianflux.co.uk

ADRIAN FLUX

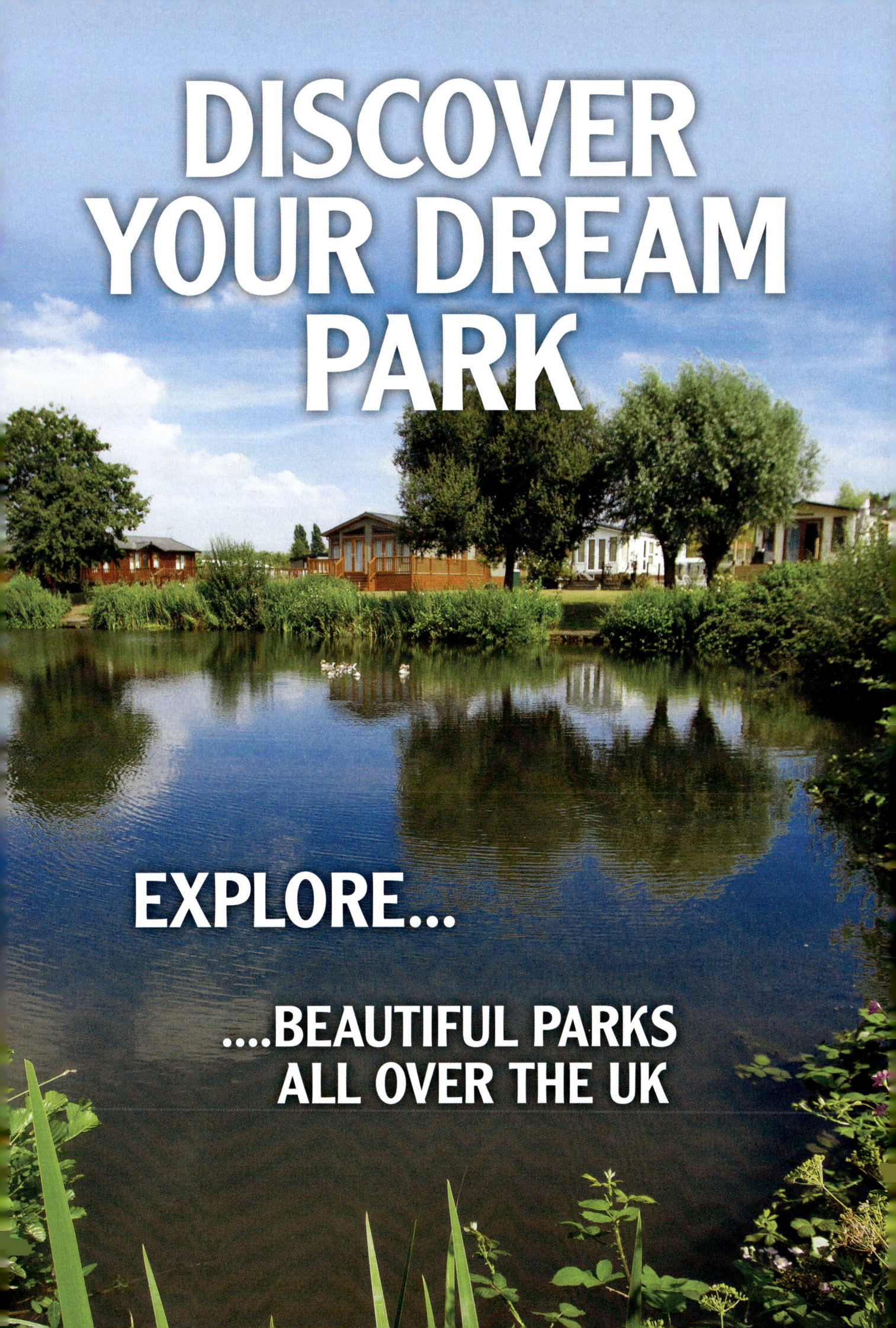

THE SPRINGS LAKESIDE HOLIDAY HOME PARK

SPRING PLANS FOR THE SPRINGS!

With 22 new holiday home plots being created this spring, now is a great time to take a close look at this park with six lakes, surrounded by the beautiful Worcestershire countryside

In beautiful Worcestershire sits a holiday home park in a gorgeous setting, with six lakes. The park is currently expanding its offering, with the addition of 22 holiday home bases. Work has already started and is scheduled for completion in the late spring.

The Springs is in the Vale of Evesham, close to the elegant market town of Pershore, which is on the banks of the River Avon and famous for its medieval abbey and Georgian architecture. Evesham and Upton upon Severn are both just six miles from the park; Worcester is 10 miles away.

Pershore is in the heart of the fruit-growing lands of Worcestershire, and it's the home of the annual Plum Festival. Apples,

THE SPRINGS LAKESIDE HOLIDAY HOME PARK

blackberries, pears, asparagus, plums, gooseberries, raspberries, strawberries and pumpkins are just some of the vast quantity of produce that is grown in these fertile lands. Fruit farming, on particular, has shaped the scenery; the orchards are quite spectacular, especially at blossom time in the spring.

EXPLORE WORCESTERSHIRE

The rolling landscape of Worcestershire lies between the Malvern Hills and the mellow-stone Cotswolds villages. One of the most spectacular of the villages is Broadway, known as the Jewel of the Cotswolds.

With The Springs as a base, there's a lot to explore in Worcestershire. We've picked out a few of the gems here… Rail enthusiasts will love the Severn Valley Railway – you can take a 16-mile steam train ride from Kidderminster to Bridgnorth. You can visit the West Midland Safari Park near Bewdley, or climb to the top of the landmark Broadway Tower, from where you can see 16 counties. And you can spend endless days exploring the quaint and beautiful villages of the Cotswolds.

THE SPRINGS

The Springs is a spacious estate, with conservation areas as well as its six lakes.

Facilities include free WiFi, an indoor swimming pool and a Members' Clubhouse that overlooks an eight-acre lake. The other five lakes offer private fishing.

The park is part of the Allens Caravans group and is the only Allens park to offer hire of lodges and twin units, which means you can get to know the park and its lovely surroundings while you are considering buying a holiday home here.

The Springs is open for 10 months of the year; the closure period is in January-February.

HOLIDAY HOMES

There's a range of holiday homes from which to choose – and Allens has its own showground (The Valley, Evesham, Worcestershire WR11 4TP) on which to display those available. Among those currently on show are a Willerby Avonmore 38ft by 12ft two-bedroom home, a Willerby Vogue lodge (42ft by 13ft), also with two bedrooms, a Willerby Juniper lodge (45ft by 22ft) with three bedrooms and a Willerby Rowan (45ft by 20ft) with two bedrooms.

Contact
The Springs
Salters Lane, Lower Moor,
Near Pershore, Worcestershire
WR10 2PD
01386 861851
allenscaravans.co.uk

WELSH HOLIDAY HOMES WITH A VIEW

NEW PLOTS AVAILABLE

Sunbeach Caravan Park offers you the choice between the countryside, mountain walks and the beach. This location is perfect for your getaways to Wales. Nestled on the coast between the Cambrian Mountains and Cardigan Bay, Sunbeach is one of the most popular caravan parks in Wales. Not only does the Park have a stunning natural backdrop, but its location is perfect if you want to go out and see what North Wales has to offer.

Caravan holidays are ideal for those wanting to relax in a tranquil spot, surrounded by natural beauty. They are also perfect for those wanting a convenient base that allows them to explore the surrounding area without having to sacrifice the luxury of creature comforts.

- Free WIFI
- Open 11 Months
- Driftwood Clubhouse with Restaurant
- Indoor Swimming & Splash Pool
- Children's Play Area
- Toddler Soft Play
- Adventure Playground
- Teenagers' Games Room
- Small Shop
- Boat Park
- Own Beach Frontage
- Sea Fishing
- Seaside, Countryside & Mountain Walks

Sunbeach Caravan Park, Llwyngwril, Gwynedd, Wales, LL37 2QQ

WWW.ALLENSCARAVANS.CO.UK
01341 250263

ARIA RESORTS

MORTGAGEABLE HOLIDAY HOMES

Aria Resorts offers holiday homes in all styles, some with hot tubs, at locations all over Britain – and, at four locations, there are homes on which you can take a mortgage!

Aria Resorts, the group which has holiday homes for sale in many desirable areas from Cornwall to Scotland, invites you to "Press pause on the day-to-day pace and discover a modern British escape where the emphasis is on providing the perfect backdrop to the gorgeous local scenery and landmarks."

All you need to do is choose the right one for your holiday home hideaway.

You'll find, at some of the Aria Resorts, luxury lodges that are exclusive to Aria. These are the newest models from leading manufacturers, with specially commissioned interior designs and, wherever possible, the option to bespoke order.

And Aria is making waves in the industry by introducing mortgageable holiday home options at four of its leading resorts.

At Aria you can expect a collection of luxury holiday homes from which to choose, all set in enviable surroundings.

Aria Resorts' activities are on offer to encourage you, in your new holiday home lifestyle, to explore the outdoors and embrace the natural surroundings with archery, woodland survival and movies under the stars, all designed to keep families entertained every time they visit their holiday home.

IN CORNWALL – MORTGAGEABLE HOLIDAY HOMES WITH HOT TUBS

With five resorts positioned along the north coast of Cornwall, Aria can offer everything from a vibrant family resort to a restful retreat in one of the most popular UK holiday destinations.

An exciting new development at Aria's flagship Cornish resort is setting a new standard for holiday accommodation in the area. Surrounded by nature and set on

An artist's impression of the rooftop lodges at one of Aria's resorts in Cornwall, Newperran

A four bed lodge, Retallack Resort and Spa

Hot tubs are available

Lodges border the lake at Retallack Resort and Spa

the edges of Retallack Resort's lakes, the latest holiday homes at Retallack Resort are architecturally designed boutique barns, with a striking floor-to-ceiling glass frontage.

Retallack Resort is just 10 miles inland of the charming fishing and foodie port of Padstow and within easy distance of many of the north coast's best beaches.

The luxurious two, three and four-bedroom boutique barns all have country views and their decking and roof terraces, complete with hot tubs, are perfect for relaxing and stargazing.

These holiday homes are fully mortgageable. Prices start from £199,950. And purchasers have the opportunity to buy for investment. A managed letting service is available.

ON THE YORKSHIRE COAST

Aria Resorts has also begun work to create an exclusive luxury lakeside resort that promises to redefine the concept of British holiday homes, at The Bay Filey, in North Yorkshire.

Deluxe country lodges cluster around a lake and nestle among picturesque landscaped surroundings at the new development, which will launch during 2020.

The Bay Filey is an especially popular choice for holiday home ownership, close to five miles of award-winning beach and a beautiful, natural landscape.

The new, gated development

ARIA RESORTS

features 55 high-specification country lodges in three different styles. Each is meticulously created to provide amazing levels of space, comfort and style, and with the option to have a hot tub.

ON THE ISLE OF WIGHT

Aria Resorts has three resorts on the Isle of Wight, with mortgageable properties available at two of them, The Lakes Rookley and The Bay Colwell.

The Isle of Wight is a magical location for a holiday home – and the pleasure and sense of adventure starts with the short ferry trip. You'll find the Isle of Wight has a lively events calendar that features sporting, music and cultural events – all of that on the island that has the enticing reputation of providing an exclusive retreat with a hint of nostalgia.

At the western tip of the Island, you'll find The Bay Colwell, home to a collection of premium two-bedroom cottages and contemporary beach houses, with spectacular sea views.

Coastal Cottage at The Bay Colwell

This serene retreat, a short stroll from a picturesque beach, is super easy for the Lymington ferry and right on the doorstep of Yarmouth's boatie scene.

The Lakes Rookley is Aria's all-action resort, at the heart of the island – and a great choice for families. Centrally located for ferry travel from the ferry from Lymington, Portsmouth or Southampton and within easy reach of many of the island's most popular attractions, The Lakes Rookley offers premium cottages and luxury lake houses to buy.

HOLIDAY HOMES FOR MANY BUDGETS

As well as mortgageable holiday homes, Aria Resorts offers a high-quality collection of static holiday homes and lodges at the majority of its resorts including those in Cornwall, Dorset, the Isle of Wight and Scotland.

In line with the requirements of today's discerning holidaymakers, the holiday homes are stylish, with all the latest models on offer, including rooftop terrace lodges.

Plots are spacious, decking is included as standard in the price and there is availability of extras such as walk-in wardrobes, integrated sound systems and the all-important wine cooler!

Lodges at The Bay Filey

The Bay Filey

Contact
Aria Resorts
0333 701000
ariaresortshomes.co.uk
sales@ariaresorts.co.uk

UK DESTINATIONS

MORTGAGEABLE HOLIDAY HOMES

70% LETTING INCOME DIRECTLY TO YOU...

SURPRISE...

Earn and enjoy!

Step away from your every day.
Discover the many benefits of buy to let holiday homes.

SEARCH 'ARIAHOMES'

Buy a holiday home for you and yours which puts money back in your pocket.

Aria Resorts' mortgageable holiday homes at a choice of UK destinations, will help you benefit from the booming UK tourist trade plus you can have some sneaky breaks too!

ARIA RESORTS

WHERE YOU WANT TO BE

ariaresortshomes.co.uk ~ 03333 701 000 ~ sales@ariaresorts.co.uk

ATLANTIC COAST HOLIDAY PARK

Words **Val Chapman**

LODGES WITH HOT TUBS!

Sheltered by dunes and close to a Cornish beach, luxury lodges with hot tubs – the perfect way to relax

On the Atlantic coast of Cornwall, a park sheltered by spectacular high dunes is now offering some very special lodges. Special not only because they're luxury lodges – but because they have hot tubs.

Imagine coming back to your lovely holiday home after a day on the beach, showering off the sand – and then slipping into your hot tub, cocktail in hand, to immerse yourself in warm-water luxury. There is surely no more perfect way to relax and unwind.

Atlantic Coast, part of the Coastdale Parks group, is a small park, quite select and very quiet, nestling under its bank of dunes that divides the park from the beach. There's a shop here (serving freshly baked bread, croissant, pan au chocolat, Cornish pasties and locally produced beers plus everyday essentials and newspapers. The park has an ambience of quality and is very neatly maintained. You could easily call this place exclusive.

Atlantic Coast is at the east side of St Ives Bay, across the bay from the artists' port of St Ives – and you can see St Ives from the

outandaboutlive.co.uk/park-holiday-homes facebook.com/parkandholidayhomeinspiration @PHHImagazine | 55

ATLANTIC COAST HOLIDAY PARK

beach, over the dunes from the park. You can also see Godrevy Lighthouse, an octagonal tower which stands 26 metres high and is a landmark for the whole of this stretch of coast.

A quick walk up and over the dunes leads you to – yes, the Atlantic coast; sunbathing, or walking on the golden sands of Godrevy and Gwithian beaches, is a joy here.

Beaches stretch for miles along the coast from Hayle to St Ives. From Upton Towans Beach close to the park, there's Mexico Towans Beach, Gwithian Beach, then Hayle Beach which sits at the estuary of the River Hayle. (The word 'Hayle' means estuary in the Cornish language.)

The natural attraction of the park and its dunes is captivating – and the sands and dunes keep children happily entertained for days. The closest area of sand to the park is a dog-free zone in the summer months but a longer walk over the dunes takes you to a year-round dog-friendly beach.

The Atlantic Coast season runs from 1 March to 4 January.

Pre-owned holiday homes are sometimes available at Atlantic Coast and there is always a selection of new holiday homes for sale.

REGAL ARTISAN LODGE £94,995

New holiday homes for sale include a Regal Artisan Lodge, a 41ft by 14ft home which has a boutique appeal, even a little apartment-like, with large patio doors and a spacious open-plan layout. Appliances include an American-style fridge-freezer, a five-burner hob and a wine cooler – and it's complete with a hot tub.

This is a holiday home designed with entertaining in mind; the dining table is large and has six high-backed chairs. It's a luxurious home, with a spacious master bedroom suite incorporating a large built-in wardrobe, an en suite shower room in two-bedroom models, plus a large vanity area with drawer space.

This lodge has a 25-year licence agreement in place. The purchase price includes the first year's pitch fee and a drain-down service (to guard against any frost damage) at the end of your first year. The price also includes full decking.

REGAL LULWORTH £49,995

Another of the holiday homes for sale is a Regal Lulworth, with panoramic front windows (or you can opt for French doors). This home has a bright, light aspect, a spacious kitchen and ample storage space. The master bedroom has a king-sized bed, built-in spacious wardrobes, a vanity area at the foot of the bed and an en suite bathroom.

Attractive stone-effect worktops in the kitchen are enhanced by the subtle pastel colour of the cupboard doors, whilst the ample storage cupboards and large open shelving add to the practicality of the kitchen.

> **Contact**
> Atlantic Coast Holiday Park
> Upton Towans, Hayle,
> Cornwall TR27 5BL
> 01736 752071
> atlanticcoastpark.co.uk

Holiday Home Ownership

Coastdale Parks
SEASCAPES · LANDSCAPES · ESCAPES
EST 1975

Coastdale Parks offers you a great selection of modern, luxurious and affordable caravan holiday homes for sale at its family holiday parks around the British coast. With all parks close to excellent beaches or popular tourist attractions, a new holiday home provides an ideal place for all the family to meet and for your leisure time to be enjoyed to the full!

We offer a number of purchase options to suit all budgets, tastes and model preferences, ranging from brand new, top of the range stylish caravans with double glazing and central heating , to good quality starter caravans - both new and pre – owned. We endeavour to find the holiday home of your dreams and we publish a regular list of all stock available for sale for immediate purchase. Alternatively, should you prefer a make and model not currently in stock then we can order that for you.

Give us a call 01502 561136 or visit:
atlanticcoastpark.co.uk (Cornwall) - garreggochpark.co.uk (North Wales)
pakefieldpark.co.uk (Suffolk) - whitbypark.co.uk (North Yorkshire)

We'll help you find your perfect holiday home.

  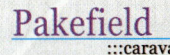  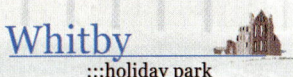

KELLING HEATH HOLIDAY PARK

NATURAL NORFOLK

Set in 300 acres of heathland and woodland, Kelling Heath is a paradise for nature lovers. It's both an adventurer's haven and a perfect retreat

Kelling Heath is a unique natural environment in north Norfolk, with beautiful stretches of unspoilt beaches, seaside towns and wildlife in abundance.

When you have a holiday home set within the natural beauty of Kelling Heath you can relax in your own home and enjoy walking through the park, taking advantage of the excellent range of facilities.

Purchase here, in this splendid location, is more affordable than you may think, with prices of holiday homes starting at £53,995. And you are also well placed to enjoy the north Norfolk coast and countryside.

The abundant wildlife and stunning landscape make the park an ideal choice for those looking for a natural environment with sustainability at its heart. With miles of woodland and heathland trails for walking and cycling, or for simply enjoying the diverse range of wildlife, the park is an adventurer's haven and the perfect retreat from busy lifestyles.

With magnificent views of Weybourne's coastline, Kelling Heath is the perfect location from which to explore the beautiful and unspoilt north Norfolk coast and countryside, a hugely desirable location with beautiful stretches of unspoilt beaches and seaside towns.

Walking through 300 acres of outstanding natural landscape does wonders for the soul and provides a tranquil retreat from the hustle and bustle of busy everyday life. It's an

KELLING HEATH HOLIDAY PARK

opportunity to relax, unwind, and appreciate the area's natural beauty.

A range of recreational and leisure facilities is on the park. These include a Health and Fitness Club with indoor pool, an outdoor pool, tennis courts, restaurants and bars, plus a village store, all located around the popular Village Square, which ensure a hive of activity.

Whatever stage in life you are at, a holiday home at Kelling is a lifestyle choice which is sure to benefit you.

Holiday homes are located on plots spread across mixed woodland, pine plantations and rare open heathland, each providing a unique and relaxing location where you can enjoy the native wildlife.

And when it comes to choosing a holiday home you will be spoilt for choice, selecting from luxury lodge-style homes to equally luxurious caravan holiday homes, with a range of pricing to make ownership of a home in this stunning location affordable. New caravan homes are available in a price range from £53,995 to £99,000. For the luxury lodges, pricing is dependent on the size and specification chosen, so it is best to discuss this with the team at Kelling Heath; then a firm quote can be provided.

As a guide, lodges are priced from £169,995 upwards.

Pre-owned holiday homes are often available, too.

A selection of show lodges and caravan holiday homes is available for viewing at Kelling Heath; the Kelling Heath website gives details of homes to view and purchase.

It's all yours!

Ownership of a holiday home at Kelling Heath entitles you not only to enjoy this unique environment but also a range of other benefits:
- Exclusive owners' website
- Dedicated Owner Services department
- Complimentary access to the Health and Fitness Club
- Discounts when dining out on the park (terms and conditions apply)
- Owner events available throughout the year
- Free use of the tennis courts

For more information call Holiday Home Sales on 01263 589900 or email holidayhomesales@kellingheath.co.uk

Contact
Kelling Heath Holiday Park
Weybourne, Holt, Norfolk
NR25 7HW
01263 589900
kellingheath.co.uk

The natural escape
FOR YOUR HOLIDAY HOME IN NORTH NORFOLK

Lodges and caravan holiday homes for sale at Kelling Heath

When you have a holiday home set within the natural beauty of Kelling Heath you can relax in your own home, enjoy walking through the park taking advantage of the excellent range of facilities. You are also well placed to enjoy the North Norfolk coast and countryside.

- A choice of fully furnished lodges
- Caravan holiday homes also available
- Choose from woodland or heathland settings
- Income if you choose to let*

Owner benefits include:
- Free membership of the Health & Fitness Club
- Special rates in the bars and restaurants
- Owner events all year

COME AND SEE FOR YOURSELF

SHOW LODGES & CARAVANS TO VIEW

*Letting arranged privately not through Kelling Heath.

Call **01263 589900** or www.kellingheath.co.uk
Kelling Heath, Weybourne, Holt, Norfolk NR25 7HW

KELLING HEATH

PARKDEAN RESORTS

YOUR NEW ADVENTURE

Parkdean Resorts offers you 62 parks, a new, specially selected range of holiday homes in five levels of specification – and an invitation: 'See where a holiday home can take you'

Every weekend is an excuse for a new adventure with a holiday home on one of Parkdean Resorts' 62 parks across the UK. This year, Parkdean Resorts, the UK's largest holiday park operator, offers this invitation: "With so much to enjoy all year round, isn't it time you saw where we could take you?"

SEE WHERE A HOLIDAY HOME CAN TAKE YOU…

From beaches to peaceful woodland retreats, whatever your pursuit of preference, there is a park for you.

Parkdean Resorts, experts in helping thousands of people realise their dream of owning a holiday home, places affordability at the core. Parkdean Resorts' new, five-tiered range features differing layers of specification and prices so you can pick the perfect dream home for your budget.

… TO BEAUTIFUL LOCATIONS

With so many unbeatable locations to choose from, Parkdean Resorts is able to offer choice in abundance. The company's 62 holiday parks are in some of the UK's most beautiful destinations – including the shores of Lake Windermere, the stunning Scottish coast and close to some of Cornwall's finest beaches.

… TO GREAT FACILITIES

An attraction of buying a holiday home on a Parkdean Resorts park is the brilliant facilities; these are parks where the focus is firmly on families.

You can relax, or keep fit, in the indoor and outdoor pools. Little ones will never tire of the parks' adventure playgrounds and will love making friends at the kids' clubs.

When it comes to evening entertainment, Parkdean Resorts has got that covered, too. From meals in family-friendly restaurants to taking in the entertainment in the parks' Showbars, there's something for everyone. When you choose ownership with Parkdean Resorts, you'll get to enjoy it all, with something new to discover each time you visit your holiday home.

… TO A NEW LIFESTYLE

As a holiday home owner with Parkdean Resorts, you'll be able to escape to holiday heaven as often

Making the dream reality

As well as offering holiday homes for sale to suit all budgets, Parkdean Resorts is able to offer various payment options* to help you spread the cost of your holiday home – with deposits starting from just 10%.

Parkdean Resorts' owner letting schemes provide a great opportunity to offset the running costs of your holiday home by letting it out when you're not using it.*

*Finance is available on selected holiday homes based on age of unit. Subject to status. Terms and conditions apply.

*Prices vary between models and Parkdean Resorts parks. Subject to availability.

*Your inclusion in our letting schemes does not guarantee that we will fill every date. Full terms and conditions of our sub-letting schemes are available from Reception on park

as you like. Many of the parks offer 12-month seasons.

Buying a holiday home with Parkdean Resorts means you'll be joining a community of like-minded owners, so it's easy to make friends, especially as owner-exclusive events take place at many of the parks.

...START YOUR JOURNEY NOW!

Ready to see why thousands of people have decided to buy a holiday home at Parkdean Resorts? Start your journey to finding your dream location and perfect holiday home by arranging an appointment at a park of your choice – call 03332076708 or go to parkdeanresorts.co.uk/ownership

The Parkdean Resorts team can advise you on facilities and location. So, whether a swimming pool is a must, or you've got a particular region in mind, the team will help you find your perfect holiday home location.

Parkdean Resorts will help you discover the park that's right for you, and arrange a viewing. Call 03332076708 or visit parkdeanresorts.co.uk/ownership to see where a holiday home could take you.

PARKDEAN RESORTS

Parkdean Resorts' 2020 model range

Parkdean Resorts' new range of holiday homes offers something for all budgets. So, whatever your priorities in terms of specification and luxury, you'll find it easy to choose your ideal holiday home from Parkdean Resort's carefully chosen ranges, made by Swift, Willerby, Carnaby, ABI and Prestige Homeseeker. Some of these holiday homes are available in a choice of sizes and layouts.

Swift Loire

Carnaby Oakdale

Swift Vendee

Start by taking a look at the Lifestyle range, where the ethos is affordability and value for money.

These are excellent starter holiday homes: the Swift Loire (bright, fun and functional), the Willerby Grasmere (amazing value for money, with central heating) and the Willerby Kelston (spacious, super-practical and great value).

A little more luxury – and still great value for a modest outlay.

Choose from the Willerby Castleton (with a dining area that's designed for media as well as meals), the Swift Bordeaux (with an open-plan layout), the Carnaby Oakdale (with seating incorporating stowaway footstools), and the ABI Windermere (with a country look).

Higher in specification and offering sumptuous holiday living.

Homes in this range are the Swift Vendee Lodge (with classical styling), the ABI Ambleside (with a window seat in the main bedroom!), the Carnaby Chantry Lodge (plush and luxurious) and the Carnaby Glenmoor Lodge (with a country house theme).

ABI Beaumont

The next step up is Parkdean Resorts' Aspire range, three models offering homes of style and sophistication. These are the ABI Beaumont (refined, with a touch of classical class in the décor), the Willerby Waverley (sophisticated, with a kitchen island unit) and the Willerby Vogue Classique (with a skylight in the main bedroom, a reclining settee and an American-style fridge-freezer).

LODGE RANGE

At the top of Parkdean Resorts' portfolio is the Lodge range, larger than the holiday homes and with luxury at their heart.

These are the Willerby Portland (with a classic country cottage feel, and beautiful pastel shades), the Willerby Pinehurst (with a traditional feel and a kitchen island breakfast bar), the Prestige Homeseeker Burleigh Coastal (with a beachy chic look and spec including a dishwasher and washing machine) and the Swift Toronto Lodge (available with a triple bunk room!).

Willerby Portland

FROM WEEKS

...TO OURS

See where holiday home ownership could take you.

Why have just one holiday a year, when every weekend is an excuse for a new adventure with your own Parkdean Resorts Holiday Home? From lodges to caravans and family-fun to rest and relaxation, we've got a home for everybody and every budget. So what are you waiting for? Take your first steps to holiday home ownership at one of our 62 parks today.

Call us now on **03332 076 708** or visit us online at **www.parkdeanresorts.co.uk/ownership**

Parkdean Resorts
Creating Amazing Memories

CLUB HOLIDAY HOMES

A HOLIDAY THAT'S READY WHENEVER YOU ARE

Holiday homes in eight locations, including Scotland, Wales, the Peak District and the Lake District, from an industry leader

Buying a holiday home to escape to whenever you choose is a significant lifestyle choice. With Club Holiday Homes, part of the Camping and Caravanning Club, you can rest assured in the knowledge that the organisation is an industry leader with over 115 years' experience, so the team knows what you want from your holiday home and how to help you to get it.

The Club has eight stunning locations across the UK for you to choose from, all in popular destinations including Scotland, Wales, the Peak District and the Lake District.

The Club's range of lodges and

A Holiday That's YOURS TO keep

YOUR HOME FROM HOME

PRIME LOCATION!
Holiday Caravan
Windermere
£41,995

MUST BE SEEN
Holiday Caravan
Alton, the Star
£29,250

SCENIC BEAUTY
Holiday Caravan
Scone
£32,995

Own your dream holiday home, from a name you can trust.

If like us you have been caravanning or holidaying in the UK for years and feel it's time to plant your feet in a place to call your own, then let us help you make it come true with Club Holiday Homes, part of the Camping and Caravanning Club.

Offering a range of static caravans on some of our most beloved Club sites, why not enjoy the natural beauty and stunning scenery of the UK. While you enjoy your very own Holiday Home, your find a community of like-minded people; sharing similar interests creating a small a community for years to come.

You can find out more about Club Holiday Homes and the stunning locations and holiday homes available, by visiting our website or speaking to a member of the holiday homes team.

www.clubholidayhomes.co.uk/locations | 024 7647 5328

CLUB HOLIDAY HOMES
FROM THE CAMPING AND CARAVANNING CLUB

DON'T JUST CALL IT *Special* CALL IT *Yours*

Own your dream holiday home,
from a name you can trust.

www.clubholidayhomes.co.uk

CLUB HOLIDAY HOMES
FROM THE CAMPING AND CARAVANNING CLUB

A *holiday* THAT'S READY *When* YOU ARE

WONDROUS WINDEREMERE

Own your dream holiday home, from a name you can trust.

As breath-taking as the lake that shares its name – our site at Windermere hosts an array of luxury lodges and stunning static caravans benefiting from environmentally-friendly facilities to match its beautiful surroundings. Conveniently located between the towns of Kendal and Windermere, as well as the varied attractions and natural beauty of the Lake District, it's the perfect holiday destination.

www.clubholidayhomes.co.uk/windermere | 024 7711 0105

CLUB HOLIDAY HOMES
FROM THE CAMPING AND CARAVANNING CLUB

static caravans are quality assured and to the highest standards. With a mix of new and pre-owned units for sale, you are bound to find the perfect holiday home for you.

Some of the Club Holiday Homes parks are detailed here.

WONDROUS WINDERMERE
This park is as beautiful as the lake with which it shares its name. Holiday Home ownership at Windermere means unmatched surroundings with excellent environmentally-friendly facilities to enjoy, along within the community of holiday home owners. Situated between Windermere and Keswick, this park is ideal for travelling to both areas, exploring the towns and villages or taking a boat across Lake Windermere to experience the incredible picturesque views.

ALLURING ALTON
Peacefully perfect, on the edge of the Peak District National Park, with excitement close by, Alton offers a wide selection of used and new holiday homes, so you are bound to find the ideal home that suits your budget and your taste. This park is perfect for relaxing breaks; with traditional market towns, railways and shopping centres, you are spoilt for choice. For walking enthusiasts, there are plenty of must-see sights and trails to enjoy again and again. And the excitement? That's because Alton is just a few miles from the amazing haven of fun and adventure that is Alton Towers.

SPECTACULAR SCOTLAND
Wild natural beauty, abundant wildlife and stunning lochs… Buying a holiday home in Scotland places you amidst some of the most beautiful scenery in the UK. With three Club Holiday Homes parks in Scotland to choose from, breathtaking lochs, magnificent mountains, rolling hills, majestic forests and dramatic coastline are guaranteed – and you'll always find new sights to be discovered.

MAKING FRIENDS
Club Holiday Homes is all about enjoying the tranquil nature of peaceful surrounding of the Club's parks and plenty of Mother Nature's most extraordinary scenery to captivate you. Imagine gazing out of the window of your holiday home, morning coffee in hand, deciding where to explore today.

Becoming a Club Holiday Homeowner means knowing you're in safe hands every step of the way to buying your holiday home, and then enjoying your favourite location for years to come. During your time at your holiday home you're guaranteed to meet and make lifetime friends among like-minded people. Becoming part of this small community allows you to relax, gather with friends, entertain family and explore the area.

PERFECT PASTIMES
Pastimes are an essential ingredient of leisure time and, amongst the stunning scenery of Club Holiday

The Club's Alton site

CLUB HOLIDAY HOMES

Home parks, you can enjoy the things you love the most. This may be a simple stroll through a local village, birdwatching, exploring nearby forestry on foot, cycling – or maybe just a quiet drink with friends. With Club Holiday Homes you can make your pastimes now-times.

YOUR FOUR-LEGGED FRIEND
Pets are welcome on all Club sites, so if you have a furry companion, you can be sure that they will be able to enjoy holidaying with you. Club Holiday Homes only asks you to keep them on a lead and not let them get up to too much mischief!

A TEAM ON HAND TO GUIDE YOU
The Club understands that purchasing a holiday home is a big decision and so the team will be on hand to guide you through the process. Location, lifestyle and the right type of holiday home for your needs are all important factors, as is affordability; the Club is transparent about the costs involved to help you make the right choice.

Licence periods range from 15 years for a new static caravan to up to 50 years for a new lodge. The length of time that the owner can occupy a home during a year varies from park to park; some up to 11 months in any 12 month period.

Site fees range from £1,500-£5,700 per annum. Club Holiday Home customers have access to a team of staff with experience in helping owners to choose their perfect holiday home. Support doesn't end once a customer has signed on the dotted line – the Club is there at every stage to guide you through your journey to ownership.

Contact
You can browse and explore special offers on the Club Holiday Homes website club-holidayhomes.co.uk, email chh.enquiries@campingand-caravanningclub.co.uk or call 02477 670 242 to begin your journey to owning a Club Holiday Home.

A holiday THAT'S READY When YOU ARE

ALLURING ALTON

Own your dream holiday home, from a name you can trust.

Truly a star, our lovely site at Alton, home to a range of static caravans, is perfect for enjoying the peace and natural beauty of the Peak District National Park and Staffordshire Moorlands. Both are ideal for walkers and lovers of the great outdoors or why not bring the grandkids along to enjoy the exciting family attractions of Alton Towers Resort, just a mile away from the site?

www.clubholidayhomes.co.uk/alton | 024 7647 5328

CLUB HOLIDAY HOMES
FROM THE CAMPING AND CARAVANNING CLUB

SEARLES LEISURE RESORT

One of the lodges in the Country Park area

A COMPLETE FAMILY RESORT!

Searles is an entire family resort on the north Norfolk coast, offering an array of leisure facilities, a choice of eateries, plus daytime and evening entertainment...

A Prestige Bella Vista, one of the show lodges at the park

Searles Leisure Resort is a family-run 'village' that has been offering holidays on the north Norfolk coast of 'Sunny Hunny' for more than 80 years. It's a five-minute walk from Hunstanton beach.

Facilities include indoor and outdoor swimming pools, a splash pool, a hot tub and sauna, a soft play area and entertainment, plus two golf courses, fishing lakes, tennis courts, a bowling green, pétanque and cycle hire.

This comprehensive resort offers something for everyone, from touring pitches to holiday homes, cabins and lodges to rent – and, of course, the opportunity

Outdoor Seating at the Fountain Sports Bar

to buy your own holiday home in this fantastic environment. The important point made here is that if you're considering buying a holiday home here, there are plenty of opportunities to stay on the resort before you buy, to experience all that Searles has to offer. And, if you buy a holiday home during your stay, you get the cost of your holiday accommodation refunded.

DINING CHOICE
Searles Leisure Resort offers an array of dining options including Smokey Jo's Restaurant, The Fountain Sports Bar and Restaurant, Harry's Fish 'n' Chips, The Cook House Takeaway,

SEARLES LEISURE RESORT

Silk Road Express Chinese, plus a poolside Catering Pod. Start your day with a full Norfolk buffet breakfast along with a wide selection of tasty additions such as pancakes, waffles and muffins. Then let the array of menu choice tempt you through the day and into the evening. Or you can enjoy cooking in your own holiday home; Searles has a supermarket for all your self-catering needs.

FITNESS STUDIO
The fitness studio is fully equipped with weights, resistance machines and aerobic exercise equipment.

BEAUTY SALON
Searles also has its own beauty salon offering a wide range of treatments and hair styling.

SEPARATE AREAS FOR HOLIDAY HOMES AND LODGES
Searles has a selection of new and pre-owned luxury holiday lodges and high-spec holiday homes for sale.
These are arranged in two areas. At the leisure resort area, holiday homes from all the major manufacturers including Willerby, ABI, Carnaby and Atlas are available.
Pre-owned holiday homes can be bought for as little as £14,995. New holiday homes start at £37,995. And Searles takes touring caravans in part-exchange.
At the more relaxed Country Park area, by the nine and 18-hole golf courses, bowls greens, fishing lakes, tennis courts and Fountain Restaurant and Bar, there are two lodge-only areas, Fairway Court and Redgate Court.

A resort that never stands still!

BEST PARK IN BRITAIN
Searles was declared the UK's champion holiday providers in the AA's prestigious awards for 2019. The resort was the overall winner in the Holiday Centre of the Year category. Awards given by the AA are based on guest reviews and a 'secret shopper' visit by the inspectors. They are regarded as the Oscars of the holiday parks industry.

The citation from the AA's award judges noted that Searles "never stands still, and every year offers something new to delight visitors seeking a truly memorable and high-quality experience. The park's success and popularity is thanks to the vision, passion and hard work of four generations of the Searle family, and their quest for ever-rising standards".

BEST HOLIDAY PARK FINALIST
Searles is very pleased to announce that the park is a finalist in the Eastern Daily Press Hoseasons Norfolk & Suffolk Tourism Awards 2020. The park says: "We are all the more grateful to find out we have been included because of nominations by our wonderful guests." Results will be announced in February 2020.

Searles Leisure Resort has two golf courses

These are perfect for relaxing and getting away from it all.
Fairway Court, by the nine-hole course, has pre-owned lodges available. The new Redgate Court area has both new and pre-owned luxury lodges available. You can even create your own bespoke lodge!
The two lodge areas share a heated outdoor pool for the exclusive use of lodge owners and their families.

HUNSTANTON
Hunstanton is a classic Victorian resort. The coast here is famous for its striped cliffs, composed of sandstone and limestone stained by iron oxide. As the only west-facing resort on the east coast, there are spectacular sunsets over The Wash.

Contact
Searles Leisure Resort
Beach Road
Hunstanton PE36 5BB
01485 536026
searles.co.uk

Ownership Opportunities
For the lifestyle you deserve

Enjoyed your holiday? If you purchase a holiday home before you leave we will refund the cost of your holiday up to £1,500.*

* Terms and Conditions apply.

Luxury Lodges

Be part of the exclusive Country Park lifestyle and own your own luxury lodge beside our 18 Hole Golf Course. All our lodges are fully furnished plus decking and brick surround.

New Lodges from:	£150,000
Pre-owned Lodges on Redgate Court from:	£98,000*
Pre-owned Lodges on Fairway Court from:	£50,000*

*Prices subject to availability.

Holiday Homes

New and pre-owned caravans are available to buy. New holiday homes are fully furnished and the price includes siting, connection, steps and alarm.

New Holiday Homes from:	£37,995
Pre-owned Holiday Homes from:	£14,995*

*Prices subject to availability.

Minimum £1500 part exchange for your tourer when purchasing a NEW holiday home

Exclusive benefits for you!

- 2 Owners and 8 Family ID Cards
- **FREE** access to Pools and Soft Play Zone
- Discounted Food and Drink at Searles
- Discounted Food and Drink at Heacham Manor
- Discounted use of 9- & 18-Hole Golf Courses

- **FREE** Golf Membership for Searles 9-Hole course (for 2 Country Park Owners)
- Discounts at Princess Theatre (Tickets and Drinks)
- Wi-Fi on Site*

*Small Fee Applies.

Visit the Sales Office or call 01485 536026
www.searles.co.uk/ownership

WILLOWBANK HOLIDAY HOME AND TOURING PARK

Lawned areas with feature landscaping

TRANQUILLITY AND NATURE

A park close to dunes and woodland where nature is a key attraction, yet within five miles of the elegant architecture and charming seafront of Southport

The Sefton coast stretches 22 miles, a tranquil landscape of beaches, dunes and woodland. It's a paradise for people who love natural, unspoiled environments – and in particular, for birdwatchers, as well as walkers and cyclists.

Close to all of this lies Willowbank Holiday Home and Touring Park, a neatly kept, peaceful park from which you can take a walk to the dunes for which this coast is famous.

Villages are nearby – Ainsdale and Birkdale – for coffees and shopping. Further afield, the cultural cities of Liverpool and Manchester are both less than an hour away. The region has a lot to offer, as we've discovered on several visits to Willowbank. We've also discovered that the park is a delightful environment. A long, imposing driveway leads from the road to the park's gated entrance. It's set in 30 acres and has its own dog walk along one edge. The park is totally level. Parking space is by each holiday home and everything is beautifully maintained. Come and see for yourself – and, perhaps, take a look around the holiday homes that

Carefully tended displays of plants are in various places on the park

Words **Val Chapman**

A Swift Champagne on a large corner plot

All roads are well surfaced and the park is totally level

are for sale here. There's typically a good selection, and sometimes pre-owned units, too. Any make of new holiday home can be sourced.

Willowbank is just five miles from Southport, a Victorian resort of elegant architecture which retains its bygone-years charm. You'll never be short of things to do here, in addition to shopping, theatre and beach walks. The Marine Lake, between the beach and the town, offers a variety of activities; you can hire motorboats and pedalos to keep everyone in the family entertained – or even take a power boat ride.

Southport also has a pier, gardens, a miniature railway and a model railway village.

Liverpool is half an hour's drive away, or you can leave your car at Ainsdale station, a short distance from the park, and take a train. Manchester is less than an hour away.

Much closer to the park are the natural assets of the region. The Sefton coastal dune system is recognised as valuable for nature conservation as well as coast protection and recreation.

In the nineteenth and twentieth centuries, pine woodlands were planted to protect the dunes, and these also serve to enhance the landscape of the area.

BIRDWATCHING

Birdwatching is a great attraction of the Sefton coastline. We turned to the region's RSPB website for advice on which species of birds you can expect to see – and the list is a long one... On the shorelines, watch for knot, sanderling, dunlin, grey, ringed and golden plover, bar-tailed and black-tailed godwit, oystercatcher, redshank, curlew, turnstone, lapwing, whimbrel, ruff, curlew and sandpiper.

Offshore you can expect to see diver, grebe, sea-duck, shearwater, auk, skua, leach's petrel and storm petrel, fulmar, gannet, common and velvet scoter, and long-tailed duck.

In the dunes and woodland, wintering siskin, crossbill, redpoll, brambling, goldcrest, long tailed tit, redwing, fieldfare and blackcap, jack snipe and water rail can be observed from late October. Snow bunting, linnet and twite are regular winter visitors.

So, grab your binoculars and scope and off you go! And, if you buy a holiday home at Willowbank, you can go birdwatching every day that you're there, if you wish!

NATURE RESERVES: DUNES

The region has a great number of nature reserves. Here are some of them...

The Ainsdale and Birkdale Sandhills Local Nature Reserve is one of the largest areas of wild dunes in Britain. It's a region of high dune ridges and valleys containing slacks. These are hollows which often contain water during winter; some provide breeding pools for natterjack toads, for which this area is well known.

WILLOWBANK HOLIDAY HOME AND TOURING PARK

The park is neatly kept

Most of the holiday homes have lovely gardens

In summer months rare flowers grow in some of the slacks. Notable are early marsh-orchid, marsh helleborine and grass of Parnassus.

Many walks cross these areas; some are circular, and all will provide fascination. Waymarked footpaths are easy to find.

WETLANDS AND GRASSLANDS

Rimrose Valley is a country park encompassing two Sites of Special Local Biological Interest, at Brookvale Local Nature Reserve and also the extensive reed beds at Fulwood Way. Wetland plants, creatures and birds plus grassland plants including southern marsh and spotted orchids, evening primrose and bugloss can be observed. And the birds? You can expect to see snipe, water rail, woodcock, dunnock and blackcap, plus breeding pairs of reed warbler, grasshopper warbler and reed bunting.

The 150-acre Hightown Dunes and Meadows Nature Reserve stretches from Hall Road Coastguard Station to the mouth of the River Alt and forms part of the Crosby Coastal Park. Habitats here are sand dunes, saltmarsh, freshwater ponds, willow and poplar scrub plus wildflower meadows.

The Ravenmeols Local Nature Reserve leads on to the Mersey Forest. The area has a wide beach, high dunes and grassland where asparagus was once grown, backed by pinewoods.

These are just some of the recognised habitat regions along this coast. You'd never be short of new places to explore from Willowbank.

And, after a day out birdwatching, walking, exploring the dunes or cycling the many lanes and tracks, you're back at your holiday home from home at Willowbank… Tempting, isn't it? We've visited Willowbank several times, in winter and summer (the park has a 50-week season) and always found it a charming place.

Contact
Willowbank Holiday Home and Touring Park
Coastal Road, Ainsdale,
Southport PR8 3ST
01704 571566
willowbankcp.co.uk

AWAY RESORTS

COAST AND COUNTRY ESCAPES

Your home Away from home! Choose from five family resorts, all with top facilities, in seaside, lakeside or forest locations

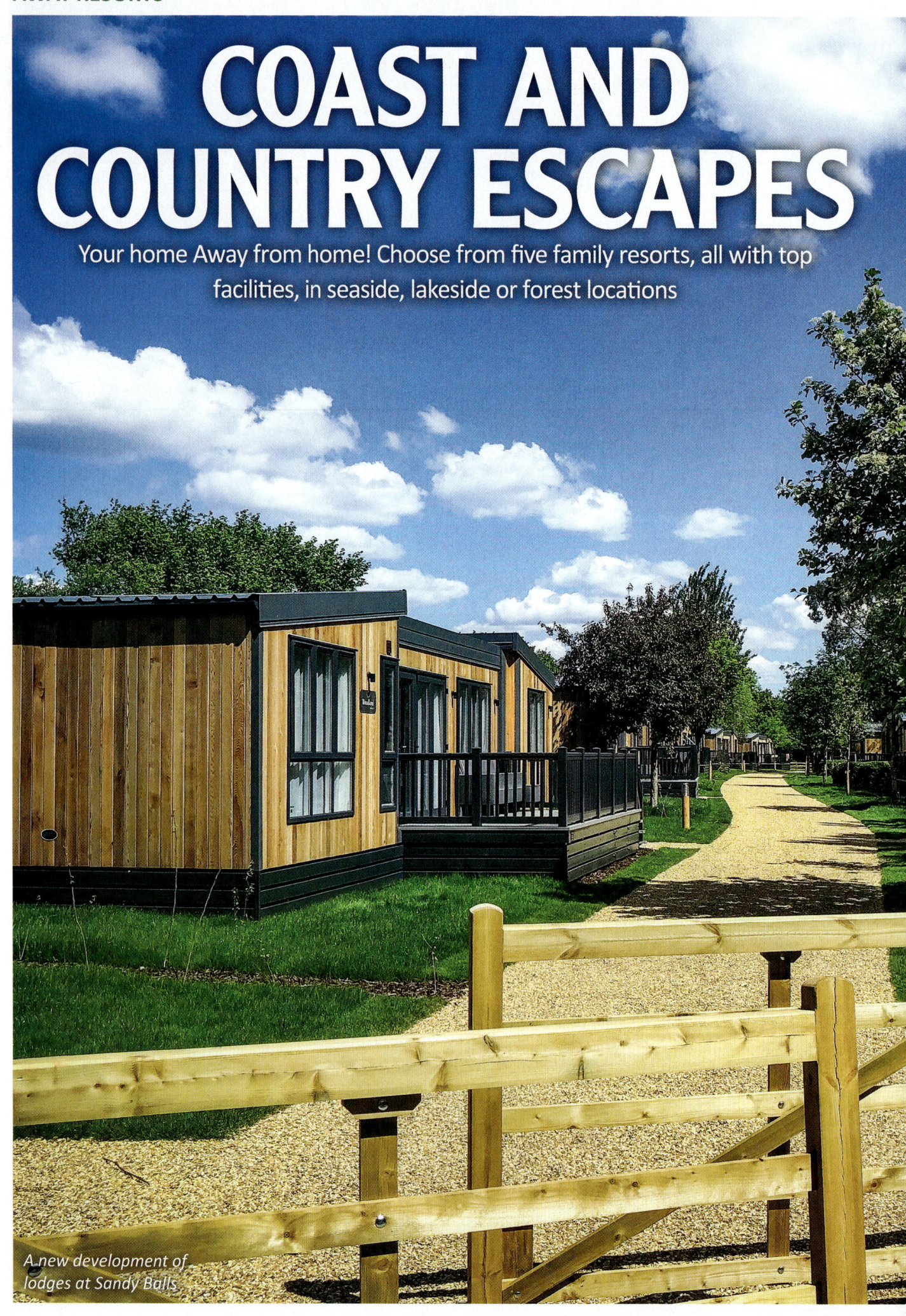

A new development of lodges at Sandy Balls

Words **Val Chapman**

Five parks in Hampshire, the Isle of Wight, Lincolnshire, north Wales and Essex, all with entertainment and superb facilities… From seaside to forest, lakeside, seclusion or full-on activity location, whatever your taste, Away Resorts has it covered.

Away Resorts has a delightful, attention-grabbing headline on its website: "Escape your everyday and leap into ours." Here's what you'll discover if you do just that….

Away Resorts are well known as brilliant places in which to hire a lodge or holiday home and have a fabulous holiday. But did you know that you can become an owner with Away Resorts? That way, you can escape the rush of everyday life and head to your holiday home whenever you can create the opportunity – and then relax, and recharge the batteries.

Events and festivals are held throughout the year at all the resorts.

THE LOCATIONS
SANDY BALLS IN THE NEW FOREST

Picture this: your own place amid the beauty of the New Forest. Cycling and walking trails directly from your doorstep, squirrels to watch, tranquillity at your holiday home when you want it, plenty of activity on hand when you don't. Explore the 120-acre estate that is Sandy Balls; woodland stretching down to the River Avon. Take your pick from indoor and outdoor swimming. Keep up with fitness in the gym that is part of the park's Leisure Club. Enjoy the hot tub and sauna here, too. Then pop into The Retreat, the park's health and beauty suite, for a massage and some top-to-toe pampering.

There's a choice of eating-out opportunities and facilities, arranged in and around a charming 'village square'. Real ale and traditional pub food is the offering at the cosy Woodside Inn. You'll also find food with an Italian flair, at the stylish Forest Kitchen restaurant. You'll find a cycle hire centre, an indoor soft play area, pool and snooker tables… All this and with the New Forest spread out before you to explore endlessly. Gardens, Beaulieu (home to the National Motor Museum and much more, the quaint port of Lymington, beaches at Bournemouth, the delightful New Forest ponies to watch… The New Forest is a paradise in so many ways.

TATTERSHALL LAKES IN LINCOLNSHIRE

Fancy a lakeside location with the tranquillity of woodland and parkland that is also a water sports centre? Tattershall Lakes is a very special place. Waterskiing, jetskiing and wakeboarding is all here for you. And fishing, too.

There's also a swimming pool, a spa and a gym, plus bars and a family eaterie. And a new outdoor heated pool is due to open for Easter. This will be the second largest outdoor pool in Lincolnshire. Also due to open at Easter is a new splash pool, giving the park three in total.

Last year the park opened a stunning £5.5m outdoor elevated bar, overlooking the waterski lake.

Tattershall Lakes even has its own (man-made) beaches, plus a High Ropes Course, for swinging, jumping (and hanging on!) fun and challenge.

If you don't yet know Lincolnshire, take it from us, this is an enchanting county, of fenland, big skies and wolds, of stately homes – and of fascination for aircraft enthusiasts. Lincolnshire is home to the Battle of Britain Memorial Flight and also the Red Arrows. These amazing aircraft fly over the park regularly so it's a free air show too!

Close to the park, there's Tattershall

Sandy Balls' Forest Kitchen restaurant

Tattershall Lakes lodges bordering the water

Indoor adventure at Tattershall Lakes

AWAY RESORTS

Castle to explore. It's a landmark red-brick castle built in the fifteenth century where open-air theatre and re-enactments are an attraction.

WHITECLIFF BAY HOLIDAY PARK ON THE ISLE OF WIGHT

An island retreat or a lively holiday centre – what's your preference? Whitecliff Bay is both of those things. So, whatever your idea of the perfect park on which to buy a holiday home, Whitecliff Bay ticks the boxes.

This is what you'll find here. You can relax on the sun terrace by the outdoor pool. You can swim rain or shine in the indoor pool, complete with flume and toddler pool. You can enjoy the park's outdoor cinema events, entertainment, mini golf, indoor and outdoor play areas... All this, and a sandy beach on your doorstep.

Eating and drinking is catered for with the Nab Bar and restaurant, plus the park's supermarket.

Whitecliff Bay is at Bembridge on the easterly point of the island. Restaurants and cafés, a pier – and the white cliffs of Culver Down are attractions here.

The Isle of Wight is very close to the Hampshire coast. You can get there by car ferry from Portsmouth, Lymington and Southampton. Discounted ferry travel is available for owners.

Whitecliff Bay's pool and beach

Holiday homes for sale

A wide range of new holiday homes and lodges is available, plus a large selection of used homes. Two, three and even four bedroom options are available. Some of the holiday homes even have hot tubs.

Away Resorts offers a subletting scheme should you wish to let out your holiday home to help offset the running costs.

BARMOUTH BAY IN WALES

There's something spellbinding about the west coast of Wales. It has a deliciously remote vibe. Yet it's not – the resort of Barmouth is here to provide all needs. Beaches and mountain scenery combine to create a wonderful region where exploration and discovery are as guaranteed as relaxation.

Barmouth Bay has direct access to a beautiful sand-and-shingle beach. It has a large indoor pool, and a new play area was installed in 2019. Cycling and walking trails lead from the park. And the backdrop to the park? That's the foothills of the magnificent mountains of Snowdonia.

MERSEA ISLAND HOLIDAY PARK IN ESSEX

Mersea Island is an idyllic holiday home location – a peaceful retreat with a captivating character. The island's expansive beaches are perfect for relaxing times and walks – and for watching windsurfers when the current, tide and wind are ideal.

Mersea Island's pool

Mersea Island is the most easterly inhabited island in the UK and is just nine miles from the city of Colchester. The island covers around seven square miles. There's a great choice of types and styles of cafés, restaurants and pubs on the island, including an oyster bar and a pizzeria. Boat trips and sea fishing trips, clay pigeon shooting and Roman history is all here on your doorstep at Mersea Island Holiday Park. There are also two farm shops on the island plus a place to buy freshly caught fish from local fishermen.

Mersea Island Holiday Park has direct access to a shingle beach. The park has an indoor swimming pool with a totally glazed cover, so it's as appealing as an outdoor pool but completely sheltered! There's an outdoor adventure playground, a clubhouse, a shop, and family entertainment during the peak season. Walking and cycling trails abound on the island.

Barmouth Bay beach

Your New Lifestyle

Ever dreamed of having your own place where you can escape to, relax and do just as you please, whenever it suits?

Whatever your into, you'll find something to float your boat at one of our amazing locations.

5 Stunning Locations to choose from...

Tattershall Lakes
Tattershall, Lincolnshire

Call 01526 348 801 for more information

Sandy Balls
New Forest, Hampshire

Call 01425 651 206 for more information

Whitecliff Bay
Bembridge, Isle of Wight

Call 01983 874 365 for more information

Mersea Island
Mersea Island, Essex

Call 01206 383 252 for more information

Barmouth Bay
Gwynedd, North Wales

Call 01341 247 350 for more information

--- **Time for a change?** ---

Already a holiday home, touring caravan or motorhome owner? Excellent hassle free part exchange offers available.

See our range of holiday homes, order your brochure and more at
awayresorts.co.uk/holiday-homes

Holiday Homes at

PREMIER LEISURE PARKS – GREENWAYS OF GOWER

SEASIDE SPLENDOUR

Imagine owning a holiday home on the coast with views of the sea. But not just by any area of coastline, the Gower Peninsula – Britain's first-ever Area of Outstanding Natural Beauty. Interested? Greenways of Gower Premier Leisure Parks has you covered

Overlooking Oxwich and Three Cliffs Bay, the award-winning Greenways of Gower offers holiday home owners spectacular views across the sea and surrounding countryside. These are rated as some of the best views of the Gower Peninsula, but you don't have to travel far to see them, you just have to walk to your window!

It's not just the views that are spectacular, the holiday lodges available to purchase on the park match the surroundings in beauty.

Currently available is the stunning ABI Harrogate, furnished to a very high standard and complete with decking, this holiday home is ready to move into and begin your seaside escape.

Also on offer is a Swift Whistler lodge, on a pitch commanding some of the best beach and countryside views of Gower, this spacious, high-quality lodge has everything you could dream of and more.

The lodges are licenced for holiday use at any time of the year.

Both lodges have a 30-year licence agreement. Both are priced at £135,000 which includes

PREMIER LEISURE PARKS – GREENWAYS OF GOWER

the first year's pitch fees.

Greenways of Gower's website sums up the 'feel' of the area perfectly: "The Gower Peninsula was designated Britain's first Area of Outstanding Natural Beauty in 1956 and it's easy to see why. Measuring only around five miles wide and little over three times this in length, the peninsula has plenty of rustic beauty and old-worldly charm…"

The Gower has ancient monuments including 30 Iron Age forts, plus legend, mystery and tales of haunted wells… "On Gower there is mystery and adventure to discover at every turn!"

Greenways is exceptionally well landscaped, not just with the flora and fauna that border the pitches but also, as it is situated on a hill overlooking the sea, every care has been made so that as many pitches as possible enjoy the fantastic views of the Gower coastline. Sitting out on your decking in the morning, enjoying a coffee and gazing across this fantastic part of the British isles, it really doesn't get much better than this!

The Gower Peninsula is the perfect place to get back to nature and Premier Leisure Parks also has two other parks in the area – Whiteford Bay and Green Meadow. The only dilemma you'll have is choosing which of these fabulous parks is the perfect one for you.

WHITEFORD BAY

Whiteford Bay Premier Leisure Park overlooks the beautiful bay. Its peaceful location is one of Gower's best-kept secrets – and it's renowned for wonderful sunsets. This is the largest of the three Premier Leisure Parks, yet it is known for the same friendly atmosphere as the group's other parks.

Nestled behind Whiteford Burrows, this hidden gem has a large adventure playground, making it an ideal choice for families. There is also a launderette and shop. The park has no clubhouse – but the Britannia Inn, with restaurant, is within walking distance, along with a village shop where you can sit in the café for home-made tea and cakes or buy local produce at your leisure.

GREEN MEADOW

Green Meadow Holiday Park is the newest addition to the Premier Leisure Park group and is now the sister site to Greenways Premier Leisure Park just down the road. This park has stunning views across the coast.

Green Meadow has its own small play area and launderette; owners at this park are welcome to use the facilities at Greenways.

All the parks offer some stunning views and all are just a short walk to a beautiful beach.

As soon as you arrive at a Premier Leisure Park you can feel the stresses and worries of everyday life disappear as your mind and body immediately adjust to the slower pace of life and the beautiful surroundings. The only dilemma you face is… deciding which of the three parks to choose!

Contact
Premier Leisure Parks
01792 391203
whitefordbay.co.uk
greenwaysleisure.co.uk
greenmeadowgower.com

Premier Leisure Parks

Affordable luxury Holiday Homes in three spectacular settings

With a choice of three stunning leisure parks all based on the glorious and renowned Gower Peninsular, Premier Leisure Parks offer three jaw dropping locations to own your perfect holiday home. A paradise you can escape to at the drop of a hat, time and time again, whenever it takes your fancy.

As soon as you arrive at a Premier Leisure Park you can feel the stresses and worries of everyday life disappear as your mind and body immediately adjusts to the slower pace of life and the beautiful surroundings. The only dilemma you face is... deciding which park to choose.

Whiteford Bay

Whiteford Bay Premier Leisure Park overlooks the beautiful bay, has wonderful sunsets and its peaceful location is one of Gower's best kept secrets. This is the largest of the three Premier Leisure Parks but shares the same intimate, friendly atmosphere as all the groups parks.

Green Meadow

Green Meadow Holiday Park is the newest addition to the Premier Leisure Park group and is now the sister site to Greenways Premier Leisure Park just down the road. The park has it's own small play area, small laundrette and also demands some stunning views across the coast. Customers of Green Meadow are also invited to use the sister site facilities of Greenways of Gower.

Greenways of Gower

Greenways Leisure Park offers holiday home owners some spectacular scenery overlooking the beautiful Oxwich Bay. Greenways has high quality holiday homes available for sale for holiday use by private owners and boasts an array of facilities for owners to enjoy.

T: 01792 391203   **E:** info@premierleisureparks.co.uk
W: www.greenwaysleisure.co.uk

KEAT FARM PARKS

Words **Val Chapman**

All three parks are open mid-February to the end of October, all have David Bellamy gold awards and are perfectly placed to explore Kent. New and pre-owned holiday homes are available.

Hawthorn Farm

QUIET QUALITY

Three quality parks in Kent, each with very different characters, all with quiet, tranquil appeal

Three parks, two on Kent's south coast and one close to the north coast, all offer a quiet quality setting for holiday homes.

These three parks are in the Keat Farm Parks group, which has its head office at Herne Bay on the North Kent coast, where there is a showground with a selection of new holiday homes available for viewing. Typically, five or six homes are on view here.

Nowhere is very far from any point in Kent. The charming city of Canterbury; Maidstone; designer outlet shopping at Ashford; history at the magnificent and fascinating Dover Castle, the exquisitely pretty medieval town of Sandwich (once a major port)... White cliffs, sandy beaches, shingle beaches...

Kent is a charming county with a lot to offer; a great place to choose for a holiday home.

HAWTHORN FARM
Four miles from Dover, this park's holiday homes are in a pretty, 28-acre woodland setting; a place that's delightful for a quiet stroll.

The park has a café and take-away plus a small shop. The park is in the village of Martin Mill.

The seafront of St Margaret's Bay is close to the park; here, you can join the Saxon Shore Way coastal footpath. And, of course, owning a holiday home so close to Dover, you can get to France

Quex Holiday Park

for a day out anytime.

QUEX

Mature trees characterise this beautiful park, at Birchington, surrounded by farmland, in east Kent. The park's café, by the reception office building, is a great place to meet up with friends you'll make on the park.

There's a delightful, secluded vibe about Quex – you really feel you are off the beaten track, yet the park is only two miles from Minnis Bay and miles of sandy beaches. It's 15 minutes from the resorts of Margate, Ramsgate and Broadstairs.

LITTLE SATMAR

High above the south coast of Kent, at Capel-le-Ferne, this small park's holiday homes are arranged in a circular pattern around what might be termed a village green.

Little Satmar

Little Satmar

This is a delightfully quiet park; during our visit the only sound was birdsong. A short walk takes you to great coastal views. Little Satmar is less than two miles from Folkestone and six miles from Dover.

Little Satmar is the smallest of the three featured here, covering just over 10 acres. Its small size gives it a secluded, escape-from-it-all feel.

The park is a short distance from the extraordinary Samphire Hoe, a piece of land actually created during the construction of the Channel Tunnel. This 30-acre site, at the foot of white cliffs, is a place to walk, observe rare butterflies and flowers and picnic, perhaps, in outstanding scenery and tranquillity.

Enjoy the Holiday Lifestyle

New and pre-owned homes are available at all of our parks

Quex Park
Birchington, CT7 0BL
Countryside Park 01843 841273

Little Satmar
Folkestone, CT18 7JF
Coastal Park 01303 251188

Hawthorn Farm
Dover, CT15 5LA
Woodland Park 01304 852658

0800 305070   info@keatfarm.co.uk   www.keatfarm.co.uk

Keat Farm PARKS — Est. 1953

CAKES & ALE HOLIDAY PARK

FAMILY HERITAGE

A family-run holiday park on the Suffolk coast with an emphasis on tranquillity and peace – and an intriguing history

Cakes & Ale is a family-run holiday park, set in 45 acres of stunningly landscaped grounds close to the Suffolk coast.

This park has a fascinating past; it's on land that was once an American air base so, as you drive around the park, you'll be taking the very same route as that once used by American P-51 Mustangs!

It's an award-winning holiday park which is family and dog-friendly, ensuring that every member of the family thoroughly enjoys their time here.

The park is spaciously designed and has everything you would expect and more, from its modern facilities to the bar and play area, and it's worth mentioning that its landscaping programme began back in 1968. In the time since then, a well-designed array of trees, hedges, shrubs and seasonal flowers have been established, combining to create a natural ambience that is only broken by the sound of birdsong.

Fascinatingly, the park takes its name from the novel by William Somerset Maugham. That novel's title was inspired by a reference in Shakespeare's *Twelfth Night* to cakes and ale being synomymous with the 'good life' – which fits perfectly with the ethos of Cakes & Ale Holiday Park!

The park has space for children to play and facilities to keep them entertained, all conveniently

Words **Val Chapman**

viewable from the bar's al fresco seating area. There are two tennis courts plus a golf practice range, a large recreation field and an adventure playground.

The Suffolk coast offers plenty to do and see and Cakes & Ale is the perfect base from which to explore; Aldeburgh, for example, an enchanting seaside town with bijou shops, art galleries and restaurants, is just over five miles from the park. This town is world-renowned because it was the home of the composer, Benjamin Britten, the founder of the Aldeburgh Festival, which takes place in June.

This is an Area of Outstanding Natural Beauty, with stunning scenery, wide beaches, wetlands rich with wildlife, ancient heaths and a number of towns and villages – beautiful Southwold and Woodbridge are within a half-hour drive.

The park is open from 1 March to 15 January. Holiday homes start in price between £30,000 and £40,000.

Cakes & Ale
HOLIDAY PARK — EST 1968

www.cakesandale.co.uk

The ideal base from which to explore the stunning Suffolk coast and countryside, or just relax and put your feet up.

An oasis of calm, where you will find some of the most relaxing Holiday Homes in Suffolk.

reception@cakesandale.co.uk | 01728 831655
Abbey Lane | Theberton | Suffolk | IP16 4TE

CARAVAN & CAMPING AWARDS 2017-2018
CAMPSITE OF THE YEAR HEART OF ENGLAND WINNER

OAKLANDS PARK

Oaklands is a mile and a half from this beautiful stretch of coast, close to Looe

Words **Val Chapman**

ESCAPE, RELAX AND ENJOY!

Take your choice of new holiday homes (and some pre-owned ones, too) on a park that's only a mile and a half from the south Cornwall coast

Two new holiday homes have arrived at Oaklands Park, close to the south coast of Cornwall. Oaklands Park, only a mile and a half from the coast, is between the amazing, pretty whitewashed ancient fishing village of Polperro and the port-resort of Looe, with its quaint shopping streets, good choice of eateries and beach.

This is a brilliant location for a holiday home, with a hinterland of lovely countryside and the spectacular Rame Peninsula to the east (a great place for coastal walks and pretty coastal villages).

The park, which has an 11-month season (from 1 March to 31 January), has stunning countryside views. It's a perfect place in which to escape, relax and enjoy your leisure time.

Oaklands Park's facilities include a small shop, laundry facilities, outdoor play areas and a dog exercise area.

The two new arrivals at Oaklands Park are an ABI Windermere and a Regal Somerton. Decking is included in the purchase price of both of these units.

ABI WINDERMERE £59,500

The ABI Windermere has lots of outstanding features including a king-sized bed and a huge dining kitchen. Its style is rustic charm integrated with modernity. Its country décor styling, featuring checked fabric and

ABI Windermere Images supplied by ABI

traditional farmhouse touches, blends with all of the luxury equipment you'd expect, including carpet and underlay throughout, an integrated fridge-freezer, microwave and USB points in the bedrooms.

This 40ft by 12ft home has two bedrooms. It comes with skirting plus a 6ft by 4ft garden store and parking space. It's centrally heated and has a piped gas supply. It has a 20-year licence agreement.

REGAL SOMERTON £62,500

This 40ft by 13ft two-bedroom holiday home is designed to convey the impression of country cottage warmth and cosiness. It has a log burner-effect fire and lots of integrated storage including a lift-up double bed and a walk-in wardrobe in the main bedroom.

The lounge features an armchair plus a three-seater sofa with pull-out occasional bed.

The kitchen is finished with rich oak units and stone-effect worktops.

Regal Somerton Images supplied by Regal

Like the Windermere, the Somerton comes with a garden store, skirting and parking area as well as decking.

There are two more new holiday homes for buyers to consider – one of them at a special offer price. That's a Swift Biarritz, at £39,500, reduced from £44,500. It's a 12ft-wide home with big patio doors and a king-sized bed in the main bedroom.

Oaklands also has a new Willerby Sheraton, at £67,500, with a country house-style living space and also with a king size bed.

In addition, there's a good selection of pre-owned holiday homes, starting at just £12,000!

Oaklands Park
escape, relax & enjoy...

Own your own luxury retreat in Looe, Cornwall

Quality, peaceful park, ideal location for coast & countryside

New & pre-owned holiday homes with beautiful views available now

Book your viewing today!

01503 262640 | info@oaklands-park.co.uk | www.oaklands-park.co.uk

RIBBY HALL VILLAGE

Lodges on the edge of the lake at Ribby Hall Village's new development

DISCOVER SOMETHING EXCEPTIONAL

With 20 spectacular new homes in an exclusive lakeside setting, Reeds Bay is the jewel in the crown at Ribby Hall Village in the Lancashire countryside

With over 120 acres of Lancashire countryside and unrivalled facilities for adults and children, Ribby Hall Village is already one of the most sought-after holiday home destinations in the north of England. Now, as it celebrates its 25th anniversary, Ribby Hall Village is unveiling the latest chapter in its story – the exclusive Reeds Bay holiday home development.

Reeds Bay will cover 20 acres of tranquil woodland-bordered countryside and have its own lake as a centrepiece. Featuring just 20 lodges, the development promises to be the perfect 'escape to the country'.

The 20 lodges are being supplied by two manufacturers, Aspire Park & Leisure Homes and Prestige Homeseeker. The holiday homes team at Ribby Hall Village has worked with the manufacturers to ensure each home is individually designed to have its own style and character. From the latest kitchens and bathrooms, right down to sophisticated sound systems, they have selected the finest interiors to ensure the pinnacle of comfort and luxury, and to make the homes highly desirable.

Inspired by nature, the stunning, architecturally designed exteriors blend perfectly with their

countryside location. From their own beautifully landscaped gardens, and rooftop terrace in many of the lodges, Reeds Bay owners will be able to appreciate the views and wander down to the lakeside in seconds.

Aspire models available are Modena, Nordica and Pasadena, and Prestige Homeseeker will be supplying the Lookout home. The properties at Reeds Bay range in price from £295,000.

Owners have on their doorstep the unrivalled facilities of the only five-star holiday village in northwest England. The sport, leisure and dining facilities offered by Ribby Hall Village are just a short stroll away from Reeds Bay. Adults can play a round of golf on the nine-hole course or visit the Health Club with state-of-the-art gym, 25-metre pool, fitness classes, sports hall, squash and badminton courts.

For children, there's a family leisure pool which has slides, interactive water features and a splash lagoon. There are two indoor soft play areas for little ones and an outdoor adventure playground. The Village even has its own interactive wildlife centre and zoo, called Wild Discovery.

In addition, there's the SPA Hotel, plus a range of eating and drinking options to suit all moods and tastes: the Italian inspired Terrazza Restaurant, the family-friendly Bar and Grill, the Tea Room, Papa John's Pizza and Takeaway and Harrison's Bar.

For more information visit ribbyhall.co.uk/holiday-homes or call 01772 672222

The first lodge on Reeds Bay

The dining-kitchen area of an Aspire Nordica lodge

20 NEW **UNIQUELY DESIGNED** HOLIDAY HOMES FOR SALE

Set in over 20 acres of tranquil countryside, Reeds Bay is the latest development at Ribby Hall Village, north west England's only five-star holiday village.

At Reeds Bay you'll discover something truly exceptional. Our 20 new uniquely designed holiday homes enjoy an exclusive lakeside setting, with unrivalled five-star facilities on your doorstep.

Our Reeds Bay homes are of the highest specification available anywhere in the UK, each one individually designed to offer the ultimate in style and luxury living.

And because Reeds Bay is only minutes from the motorway network, escaping to your dream home couldn't be easier.

**Call our dedicated sales team on 01772 672222
or email sales.enquiries@ribbyhall.co.uk**

Reeds Bay, Ribby Hall Village, Wrea Green, Nr Blackpool PR4 2PR
www.ribbyhall.co.uk/holiday-homes

THE GRANGE COUNTRY PARK

YOUR PLACE IN CONSTABLE COUNTRY

Surrounded by the views that inspired the painter, John Constable, and put Suffolk on the art world map, a park that offers you the opportunity to find your own piece of paradise in beautiful Constable country

With luxury at an affordable price, a great community spirit, a stunning countryside setting and comprehensive facilities, The Grange Country Park is one of East Anglia's best kept secrets.

The park is an exclusive and mature development in a peaceful and picturesque location on the Essex-Suffolk border, at East Bergholt, near to Colchester.

There are spectacular views of the countryside which inspired nineteenth century Suffolk painter, John Constable.

The park is situated close to many attractions such as Flatford Mill, Clare Castle Country Park and Colchester Zoo – and the stunning Suffolk coastline is just a short drive away.

Whether you are a first-time holiday home buyer or you are looking to upgrade to a new holiday home, The Grange invites you come along and see what there is on offer. Numerous show homes are at the park for you to view, allowing you to browse around the different models from manufacturers of both luxury lodges and stunning holiday homes.

There are comprehensive facilities at The Grange Country Park. These include an outdoor heated swimming pool, a barbecue area, a play area and a newly refurbished clubhouse with a bar and a restaurant known for its first-rate home-cooked meals. And, being situated in the beautiful Suffolk countryside, there are many wildlife trails for lovely long walks.

Some families have owned homes on the park for more than 50 years and many more have been with the park for 20 years or more. With an excellent array of facilities, the park's community spirit and the fact that the park is open for 11 months of the year (February to December) it is easy to see why owners remain with Grange Country Park for so long. With brand-new holiday homes starting from just £29,995 and finance packages available, now is the ideal time to come and take a look around this beautiful park and find your new home away from home.

For more information go to thegrangecountrypark.co.uk or telephone 01206 298567.

The Grange
COUNTRY PARK

- A 14 acre leisure park set in a picturesque countryside location in Suffolk
- Outdoor heated swimming pool
- Clubhouse with bar
- Children's play area
- Restaurant
- Country walks and local pubs on your doorstep
- Dogs welcome
- Homes fully furnished
- Finance available
- Prices start from £29,995

A range of luxury holiday homes available

01206 298 567
STRAIGHT ROAD, (EAST END ROAD), EAST BERGHOLT CO7 6UX
www.thegrangecountrypark.co.uk

DULHORN FARM HOLIDAY PARK

A HOLIDAY HOME ON A FARM!

In splendid Somerset, close to the coast and with a lovely view – a family holiday home park on a working farm

Farm walks, a fishing lake, table tennis, adventure play areas – and lots of space, all with the view of Brent Knoll, one of the highest points in Somerset; Dulhorn Farm Holiday Park is a very special place.

It's conveniently five minutes from the M5 – it's also just a few minutes' drive from the sands of Weston-super-Mare.

This quality park is on a working farm – beef and sheep – and the farm trails take you along field edges from where you can take a look at the beef herd, complete with the handsome resident bull.

Dulhorn Farm is best known as a holiday park for touring caravans, motorhomes and tents – and we've stayed here many times. There's another facet to this enchanting place – you can buy holiday homes here. It's an idyllic location for your weekends and holidays, in splendid Somerset; a base for never-ending explorations of the coast and countryside.

You can get a flavour of what's all around your holiday home from the vista that awaits walkers at the top of Brent Knoll, 137 metres high and not an arduous venture.

From here, there are splendid views of the Polden Hills to the south, Glastonbury Tor to the east, the Mendip Hills and Cheddar Gorge to the northeast, the Bristol Channel and Wales to the west and the Quantock Hills to the southwest.

This is a family-owned park

Image John Chapman

Words **Val Chapman**

where the focus is very much on families. Tractor-trailer rides take place during school holidays. There is a large sports field with football nets and a basketball net, two adventure play areas and plenty of space for children to run around and play safely.

In addition to the seaside attractions at Weston and Burnham-on-Sea, the park is within a short distance of several nature reserves and National Trust sites including Uphill Nature Reserve and the National Trust sites of Brean Down, Sand Point and Middle Hope. For birdwatchers there's the Somerset Wetlands areas of Westhay and Avalon Marshes. From the park it's also a short drive to the historic city of Wells (the smallest city in England) plus Cheddar Gorge, the famous Cheddar caves and also the Wookey Hole Caves, which is a brilliant family attraction.

The park is open for 11 months of the year (closed between 9 January and 9 February).

Holiday home to see

At present there's a show home available for sale at Dulhorn Farm. It's a Willerby Avonmore, 38ft by 12ft. The layout gives you a kitchen-diner, large lounge, a main bedroom with en suite and a twin room. The price includes the first year's plot fee of £3,480, plus skirting and decking. The plot has a lawn area and space for a shed if desired.

A warm welcome awaits...

... at Dulhorn Farm Holiday Park

We are family friendly holiday park which offers spacious grass and hardstanding fully serviced pitches non electric and electric hook-up in our well-kept, level fields with excellent views of the Mendip Hills and Somerset countryside. We have four fully equipped self catering cottages on site sleeping between two and six people. Tents, touring caravans, campervans and motorhomes are all welcome. We have three play areas plus an undercover marquee games room and a large sports field with football nets, a basketball net and plenty of space for children to run around and play safely. As we are a working farm there are always some animals to see too, including our Highland and Belted Galloway cows, and throughout the high season we offer tours of the farm on our tractor and trailer rides which are always very popular.

Dulhorn Farm is a pet friendly holiday park. We have dog walks on site, as well as other walks that offer peace and tranquillity and the opportunity to spot wildflowers and nature. The nearby village of Lympsham where you will find a village shop and Post Office.

- **Seasonal pitches**
- **Part-seasonal pitches**
- **Caravan storage**
- **Rallies welcome**
- **Fishing lake**

Dulhorn Farm Holiday Park, Weston Road, Lympsham, Weston-Super-Mare BS24 0JQ
T: 01934 750 298   E: dfhp@btconnect.com   W: dulhornfarmholidaypark.co.uk

KINGFISHER HOLIDAY PARK

A CANALSIDE CENTRE OF ACTIVITY

Plenty of family facilities plus fishing, a café and pubs nearby – and a profusion of attractions within easy reach

In the Staffordshire countryside, at the junction of two canals, sits a holiday home park with facilities including an indoor swimming pool, fishing and a café.

Kingfisher Holiday Park has tennis courts, crown green bowling, a play area, a games room – and free fishing on the lake adjacent to the park.

Walking pleasure is guaranteed here, with lakeside and nature reserve paths.

There's a pub on the canal bank by the park's entrance, and three more pubs plus a takeaway are in the nearby village of Alrewas.

The Canalside Café has both indoor and outdoor seating, on decking featuring comfortable rattan-style furniture and overlooking the canal and pool. Breakfast baps and a wide selection of mail meals, plus cakes, are on the menu.

The park is brilliantly located for a range of day-out destinations including Alton Towers (30 minutes away) and Drayton Manor Theme Park (15 minutes away). Within a 45-minute drive are Stratford-upon-Avon, Warwick (and castle), the Black

Country Living Museum, Cadbury's World and Twycross Zoo.

Walkers will be pleased to know that the heart of the Peak District is half an hour away. The spectacular Heights of Abraham is 30 minutes from the park and you can be in Dovedale in 40 minutes. Closer to the park is a paintball centre (five minutes), a karting track (two minutes) and Tamworth Snowdrome, for

skiing, snowboarding, tobogganing and skating (15 minutes).

Holiday homes are in a variety of price ranges and sizes. New homes start at £34,995. Pre-owned holiday homes are often available too, starting at around £13,950.

If you want to thoroughly get to know the park before you buy a holiday home here, you can 'try before you buy', by hiring a holiday home for a week or a three-night break.

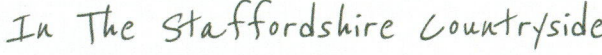

Kingfisher Holiday Park Is Situated Close To The Village Of Alrewas In The Staffordshire Countryside

About the Park

Kingfisher Holiday Park offers non residential holiday homes for sale - check the website for details. On the park we have an indoor swimming pool, tennis court, crown green bowling, an outdoor play area and a games room for the children, whilst for adults we have free fishing on Fradley Pool. You can also enjoy a stroll around the lakeside walk and Nature Reserve.

The Swan Inn is situated on the canal bank near the park entrance, whilst the nearby village of Alrewas can cater for your everyday needs with no fewer than 3 pubs, a takeaway as well as other shops. Our onsite Cafe offers lovely home made food and snacks.

The indoor swimming pool

View of the park

View of the park

KINGFISHER HOLIDAY PARK
One of the best caravan parks in staffordshire!

Fradley Junction, Alrewas, Staffs, DE13 7DN
T: +44(0)1283 790407
E: mail@kingfisherholidaypark.com
www.kingfisherholidaypark.co.uk

A HAVEN IN THE PEAK DISTRICT

With outdoor pursuits, brilliant family days out and historic houses, there's plenty to do in the Peak District – and a holiday park that could be your perfect base

Newhaven Holiday Park has been in the same family's ownership for over 50 years, through three generations. Throughout that time the focus has been on creating a peaceful environment on an immaculately kept park The latest owner, Kim Rockingham, continues this ethos. She has invested – and plans to continue to do so – to maintain Newhaven's peak status.

The park is surrounded by mature

Holiday homes for sale

There are currently two new holiday homes available. One is a 2020 Willerby Linwood, light and bright with full-height French windows, set on an extra-large plot. The Linwood is priced at £38,750 including all connections and 2020 site fees.

Soon to be available is a Swift Burgundy in a prime south-facing position at the top of the park, overlooking the natural beauty of some of the Peak District's farmland. This unit is priced at £39,500.

Newhaven also occasionally has pre-owned holiday homes coming up for sale throughout the season. In addition, the park is happy to discuss individual requirements and can order a holiday home to your own specification when a pitch becomes available.

woodland and farmland and is half way between Ashbourne and Buxton, perfectly located to explore the moorland plateaux, spectacular ridges and natural springs of the Peak District National Park, which is an area of dramatic natural beauty on a breathtaking scale.

There's so much to see and do in the beautiful Peak District, whatever your pursuits of choice. Take your pick from family days at the nearby Alton Towers for the thrill-seekers, active days spent on anything from horseriding to potholing, or exploring the history of this lovely region at one of the many historic houses, such as Chatsworth House, there is something for all tastes.

FAMILY OWNED HOLIDAY PARK IN THE HEART OF THE DERBYSHIRE PEAK DISTRICT

Surrounded by mature woods & farmland, this family owned holiday park is the perfect base for exploring the spectacular Derbyshire countryside.

With a 10 month season, immaculately maintained grounds & facilities & a well-stocked shop, Newhaven is a quiet & peaceful Park.

BRAND NEW STATIC HOMES CURRENTLY FOR SALE

2020 SWIFT BURGUNDY
available March
- 32' x 12' 2 bedroom, south facing property, in a prime position at the top of the Park with far reaching views across farmland.
- £41,750 including all connections & no site fees to pay until 2021

2020 WILLERBY LINWOOD available immediately
- 32' x 12' 2 bedroom property on an extra-large plot with lovely views across the Park to the countryside beyond
- £36,750 including all connections & no site fees to pay until 2021

- If we don't currently have what you are looking for, we would be happy to discuss your requirements for future availability.
- Second hand holiday homes come up for sale throughout the season. If you would like to be notified when they do, get in touch & we will let you know as soon as a suitable unit comes available.
- We do, on occasions, allow owners holiday homes to be bought on to the site (subject to age & condition).

For more information:
telephone 01298 84300 | hello@newhavenholidaypark.co.uk

WHITEHILL COUNTRY PARK

DEVON DELIGHT!

A new development of luxury lodges on an award-winning park with a restaurant, bar and pool, plus private woodland trails

In the rolling hills of south Devon, yet just a short distance from the coast, lies a holiday park where a new development is taking place. Show homes are arriving this spring at Whitehill Country Park, where the new development, called Orchard View, will host just 14 luxury lodges.

Orchard View is a hilltop setting, overlooking the park's Great Orchard and Bluebells Woods.

With exceptionally designed interiors and high-quality finishes, the range of holiday homes is guaranteed to provide you with a relaxing home away from home for years to come.

The new area has a gated entrance, private parking and beautiful landscaped grounds – and owners here have the opportunity to add a hot tub.

From the park, it's just a short stroll to the charming village of Stoke Gabriel on the Dart Estuary. This picture-postcard village, just inland of the 22-mile stretch of coast known as the English Riviera, is one of Devon's hidden gems, with a mill pond and a quay that's perfect for crabbing, plus pubs, cafés, ancient cider orchards and a 1,000-year-old yew tree.

If you are looking for culture, cafés and great coffee, head to the quaint riverside town of Totnes or discover the historic port of Dartmouth. The area offers a wealth of outdoor pursuits to discover, from walking the South West Coast Path to paddleboarding around the bay. If you dream of spending more time in the great outdoors, Whitehill Country Park is a brilliant base for your adventures.

Whitehill Country Park offers a range of facilities housed in the charmingly restored barns and farm buildings. You can relax beside the outdoor pool, or explore the private woodland trails. Plus, with a shop, indoor soft play area, amusements, bar, restaurant and takeaway, everything you could need is close at hand. As a dog-friendly park you will also find a spacious exercise area and even a doggy shower. And it just gets

> **Another award!**
> Whitehill Country Park is the winner of the Gold Holiday Park of the Year award in the English Riviera Tourism Awards 2019. This award follows a long list of accolades won by the park.

Show homes

New show homes are arriving at Whitehill Country Park this spring. Among them is the stunning Prestige Homeseeker Glass House, pictured here. This awesome creation is characterised by high ceilings, an abundance of windows, two rooflights over the lounge, one over the kitchen and two in the main bedroom. It has an amazing interior design which marries industrial chic with comfort and uses lots of textures including reclaimed wood. The kitchen has an island unit with a 24-bottle wine cooler. The Glass House's elevated front line was inspired by yacht design.

Other new arrivals include a Pathfinder Tuscany and a new model for 2020, a Pathfinder Tor.

better, as the park also looks forward to the addition of a new indoor swimming pool and leisure facility, set for completion in 2021/22.

In the summer months, you'll find a varied programme of live music, family entertainment and daytime activities. Whether you want to join in the fun, take a peaceful stroll in the private woodlands or simply relax and enjoy the views from your sun deck, it's all here.

Discover Your Dream Retreat in the Beautiful South Devon Countryside

Luxury Lodge Holiday Homes
Available Now from £95,000

- Award-Winning Family Park
- Peaceful Countryside Location
- Heated Outdoor Pool
- Onsite Facilites & Entertainment
- Letting Opportunies
- Selection of New & Pre-Owned Lodges
- Dog-Friendly

For further details and to arrange a viewing
Call 01803 782338 Visit whitehill-park.co.uk

Whitehill Country Park

Find Us Whitehill Country Park, Stoke Road, Paignton, South Devon TQ4 7PF

BEAUTIFUL SOUTHWEST BORDERLANDS

Nestled on the border between Devon and Cornwall is Lufflands Caravan Park, a delightful rural escape with the whole Atlantic coast on its doorstep.

If you've already chosen the South West as your destination for your holiday home, but you're not sure whether to choose Devon or Cornwall, then Lufflands Caravan Park offers the best of both worlds. Lufflands is a small, family-run holiday park that specialises in the peace and tranquillity that we all seek as an escape from the hectic pace of modern life.

Just 10 minutes north of the market town of Holsworthy and also within a 20-minute drive of the delightful resort of Bude, Lufflands is where you can begin your transformation from weekday to holiday.

The park is set in eight acres and is surrounded by forest and farmland, providing a perfect rural retreat from the everyday rat race, yet also with plenty on the park to offer holiday home owners.

It has a year-round licence, a huge exercise field for your four-legged family members and the Lufflands Bar, which is open up to four days a week during the main season and at weekends during quieter times. The bar not only offers tipples to suit every taste but also a selection of home-made meals that you can enjoy in the bar or as a takeaway to take back to your holiday home.

There's also plenty to keep the

Lufflands is a dog-friendly park!

younger members of the family entertained, with a large selection of games and equipment available. From football to cricket to table tennis, there's plenty to do and plenty of space to do it in – the perfect environment to put down those mobile phones and tablets and enjoy getting outside.

This unspoilt area of Devon really has something for everyone, from the sand and surf of the award-winning beaches at Bude and Widemouth Bay, to the sumptuous delights of dining at one of Padstow's many excellent restaurants, superb golf courses throughout the area, the fantastic walks Dartmoor has to offer, coarse fishing at a choice of lakes or, for sea fishing enthusiasts, the entire north Cornish coast is on your doorstep.

With so much to do, or spending time enjoying doing absolutely nothing, Lufflands is a beautiful place to spend your leisure time. You can relax, reset and recharge in this stunning part of the west country!

PEACE & TRANQUILITY IN THE HEART OF THE DEVON COUNTRYSIDE

- Our pet friendly, family owned and run exclusive caravan holiday park offers the personal, friendly touches that make it your home from home! Perfect rural setting to explore both North Devon and Cornwall countryside. Looking for a regular place to holiday for you and your family? We offer static caravan holiday homes for sale with a 12 month holiday season!
- Close to Award Winning coastal town of Bude with its stunning beaches and sea pool.
- Brand new and pre-owned homes are now available for viewing; visit our Holiday Home Ownership pages to see what we currently have to offer.
- The perfect time and place to make dreams come true and make special memories happen; investing in quality of life for many years to come!
- Spend a few days at our park to explore the area, the park and see if it could be the place for you....

Lufflands CARAVAN PARK

LUFFLANDS CARAVAN PARK, SOLDEN CROSS, HOLSWORTHY, DEVON, EX22 7PJ
T: 01409 241 426 E: HOLIDAYS@LUFFLANDS.COM W: LUFFLANDS.COM

GOLDEN SQUARE AND YORK MEADOWS CARAVAN PARK

YORKSHIRE TRANQUILLITY

Two idyllic holiday parks set within breathtaking tranquil landscapes

For unrivalled Yorkshire scenery Golden Square Caravan Park, set within the superb North York Moors, and York Meadows Caravan Park, nestled in the tranquil splendour of the Howardian Hills and Vale of York, are perfect places to unwind and relax.

Both parks offer a great selection of new and pre-loved luxury holiday homes. Any new model can be sourced, from suppliers including Willerby, Carnaby, Pemberton, Swift and Atlas. Whether you buy outright or on finance, there is a purchase option to suit you.

GOLDEN SQUARE
A friendly, family-run park, Golden Square has outstanding views across farm, forest and moorland. Laid out across three levels, there is a spacious and relaxed feel. Golden Square is perfect for families, with plenty to do for children on and off the park. With outdoor and indoor play areas, crazy golf and a football field, there is ample to keep everyone entertained.

Beyond the park there is a good selection of sporting and recreational facilities on offer in the local area, including country walks, pony trekking over the moors, fishing

For more information visit goldensquarecaravanpark.com

YORK MEADOWS

Set in an idyllic location, surrounded by rolling farmland, York Meadows, at Sheriff Hutton, offers an ideal get-away location.

The park is situated in a perfect area to explore the history and charm of the city of York, or perhaps one of the greatest private residences in Britain, Castle Howard stately home, just five miles from the park.

In addition, the coastal areas are not far away, with something to offer for all the family, or you can get away from it all and get back to nature, exploring the magnificent scenery of the North Yorkshire Moors.

For more information visit yorkmeadowscaravanpark.com

lakes, golf courses and even gliding at Sutton Bank.

Golden Square is well suited for exploring all that North Yorkshire has to offer; from museums and castles to theme parks and farm parks, there is something for everyone. The park was recently awarded five stars from both Visit England and the AA.

Discover Your Luxury Holiday Home
Stunning views and idyllic surroundings
Both parks offer pre-loved and NEW holiday homes

Arrange a viewing today

Golden Square Caravan Park
Helmsley, York YO62 5YQ
www.goldensquarecaravanpark.com
01439 788 269

York Meadows Caravan Park
Sheriff Hutton, York YO60 6QP
www.yorkmeadowscaravanpark.com
01347 878 508

SMYTHAM HOLIDAY PARK

NATURAL DEVON

Visit the magic of Smytham Holiday Park to relax and unwind in the heart of North Devon

Nestled in its own secluded and tranquil valley, the 33 acres of Smytham Holiday Park is the perfect place to relax and unwind away from the bustle of everyday life.

Situated in the parkland of a seventeenth century manor house, this family-run park boasts open landscaped lawns, ponds and natural woodlands – a paradise for nature lovers. From herons, kingfishers and buzzards to rabbits, hedgehogs and badgers, watch out for the abundance of wildlife that could be passing your holiday caravan to say hello.

Surrounded by stunning countryside views, it is obvious to see why the area of North Devon, in which Smytham is located, is a UNESCO Biosphere Reserve. With beautiful Devon beaches only eight miles away and the three National Parks of Dartmoor, Exmoor and Bodmin within easy reach, exploring Devon has never been easier for couples, families and friends.

Whether you wish to stay on park and lounge on the poolside sun terrace, take a splash in the pool (open May to September), soak up the sun on your decking or explore the local area by car, on foot or by bike, Smytham offers something for everyone. With direct access to the popular Tarka Trail where you may (if you're lucky!) be able to spot a frolicking otter or two, then Smytham is the place to be for cyclists and walkers alike. The open spaces and children's play area and games room provide hours of entertainment for the younger ones. For those who are slightly older, there is an on-site bar, Smythies' Bar, which is open during those busier school holidays.

Smytham Holiday Park offers both new and previously owned holiday caravans along with developed pitches to site a holiday caravan of your choice. The park's showground has caravans on display; however, caravans of any kind can be ordered especially for you.

FUN FOR THE WHOLE FAMILY

Grandparents, parents, children, the family pet and extended family are all welcomed at Smytham, making memories to last a lifetime. With the three-acre dog walking field and a dog shower, your beloved pet will feel pampered during your stays. From a table tennis match in the games room to a rounders game in the valley, at Smytham there are endless opportunities for quality family time. Equally, in our tourist information shed there is information on local attractions such as The Big Sheep where you can take in the sheep races, The Milky Way, The Wildlife and Dinosaur Park and The Lynton and Lynmouth Cliff Railway. For those of you who like gardens, RHS Rosemoor Gardens is just 5 minutes by car.

If you are wishing to find a calm and quiet park for your holiday caravan, this park, achieving a Gold David Bellamy Award for Conservation for 19 consecutive years, is the park for you. So why not come and see the magic of Smytham for yourselves?

Smytham Holiday Park

A rural retreat in the Heart of North Devon within easy reach of beaches, Dartmoor & Exmoor. Relax in your new or pre-owned holiday caravan. Holiday whatever the season with loved ones and your family pet. Have adventures, make moments that matter and create memories to last a lifetime.

- Outdoor pool
- Family bar
- Children's games room
- Shop
- Dog Walks
- Access on to Tarka Trail cyclepath

www.smytham.co.uk | info@smytham.co.uk
Little Torrington, EX38 8PU | 01805 622110

PREMIER PARKS 2020
The finest campsites, independently assessed

INSPIRATION

GADGETS AND GIZMOS

Music, heating, lighting and even lawn mowing can all be controlled remotely. Whether yours is a park home or holiday home, you're sure to love these smart devices

Electronic wizardry inspires us all. Whether we need a particular device is of course questionable. Whether we want it – just because we can – is quite another matter.

We review some amazing items here, all in theory designed to make life easier. But the real appeal surely rests with our innate desire for all things techy. From the practicality of remote heating controls and security cameras to devices that mow your lawn and make your coffee, gadgets and gizmos are designed to enrich our lives. All of these are applicable to both residential park homes and holiday homes.

Words **Iain Duff**

AMAZON ECHO ▶
£89.99 | amazon.co.uk

Invite Alexa into your home and instantly make your life much smarter. In simple terms, Amazon Echo is a voice-activated speaker with WiFi and Bluetooth compatibility and Alexa is the digital assistant who "lives" inside. But the word speaker really only tells a tiny part of the story. From the comfort of your armchair, you can instruct Alexa to play music, make phone calls, set alarms and timers, answer questions and control smart home devices… Ask for a song, artist or genre from your music streaming service… Play audiobooks, tune into radio stations, get news updates and even manage shopping lists… You'll soon wonder how you managed to get by without Alexa's help!

▲ ROKU STREAMING STICK+
£59.99 | roku.com

This little gizmo is a pocket rocket – letting you stream thousands of paid-for or free TV channels like Netflix, BBC iPlayer, Prime Video and NOW TV in vivid 4K Ultra HD. The voice remote control allows you to turn your TV on and off and adjust the volume, as well as letting you search the channels to find out where you can stream shows for free, or at the lowest cost. It's portable, too, so you can take it with you when you're away.

◀ FITBIT ARIA 2 SMART SCALES
£99 | fitbit.com

Smart scales are really nothing new… Back in the day we had talking weighing machines that told you your weight. These days, smart scales supply you with all the data you need to help you tailor your weight-loss plan, linked with fitness apps like Fitbit, Apple Health, and Google Fit. The Aria 2 measures weight, body fat percentage, lean mass and BMI and syncs the stats automatically to your Fitbit, letting you track your progress.

TILE MATE ▶
£22.99 | thetileapp.com

If you're anything like us, you probably spend a fair chunk of your day searching for things you've lost, or "misplaced", as we prefer to call it. Tile Mate is the answer. You simply attach it to your keys and, when they inevitably go walkabout, call it from your smartphone to make it ring. The app also remembers the last time and place it saw your Tile, so if you left it somewhere, you'll always know where to look. And if you can't find your phone, double press the button on your Tile Mate to make your phone ring. Tiles last a whole year without needing to be charged.

◀ BOSCH SMART HOME PLUG
£54.95 | bosch-smarthome.com

How on earth does something as apparently simple as an electrical plug become "smart"? Well, basically these gadgets let you control "non-smart" home appliances from your phone or with a voice assistant. For example, it allows you to switch table lamps on and off if you are away from home for a while, and want to give the impression that someone is in. Or you can program it to turn on your coffee maker before you get up so it's ready to go when you walk into the kitchen in the morning. With the use of an app or a smart home device, you can switch the plugs on or off remotely. The Bosch Smart Plug will connect any electrical device you plug into it to the Bosch Smart Home System and this lets you see the power consumption of the devices and program them.

INSPIRATION

◀ FLYMO 1200 R ROBOT LAWNMOWER
£500 | flymo.com

Have you been letting the grass grow beneath your feet recently? Don't worry, a robot lawnmower can do all the work for you – and, as they used to say, it's a lot less bovver than a hover. Flymo's robot mower will zip around the garden, leaving you to sit back and relax and maybe enjoy a cool drink or two, as it gets on with the job at hand. All you have to do is install the wire boundary that keeps the little critter on the grass.

▼ ARLO PRO 2 SECURITY CAMERA SYSTEM
£569.99 | arlo.com

If you spend a lot of time away from your park home, protecting it from intruders is important. This device is especially appropriate for holiday homes, too – which, by their nature, are only occupied for part of the time. A security camera that you can monitor from your smartphone will give you peace of mind. The Arlo Pro 2 lets you view live high-definition footage, no matter where you are in the world. It has sound and motion sensors that will send you alerts if they're triggered. You can also set an alarm to sound on the base station when motion is detected. The camera can either be set up inside or outside your park or holiday home and will automatically switch to night vision after dark. The system includes two rechargeable cameras and a base station.

" *A security camera that you can monitor from your smartphone; you can view live footage no matter where you are in the world* "

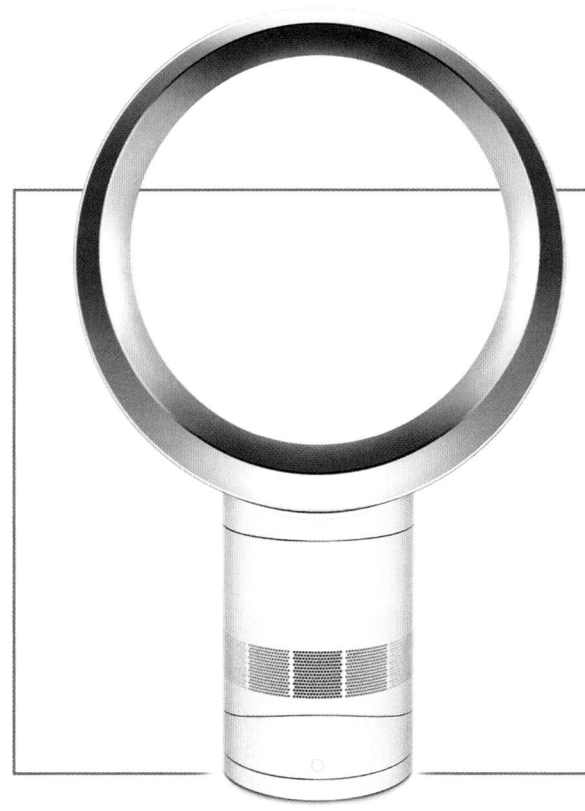

◀ DYSON COOL DESK FAN
£249 | dyson.co.uk

For style and elegance, Dyson fans are hard to beat. They are a design classic, and will really add something to the appearance of your home. Thankfully, it's not style over substance... They work really well, too. Quietly powerful, using jet engine tech, they will keep your living room or bedroom pleasantly cool in the height of summer, without the annoying drone you get from most other fans. Dyson fans are also bladeless – making them easier to keep clean and safer if there are children or pets around. Like most Dyson products, they come with a premium price tag but the Cool desk fan, designed for smaller spaces, is possibly the best value in the range at £249.

HIVE ACTIVE HEATING THERMOSTAT ▶
£179 | hivehome.com

With a smart thermostat, gone are the days of returning to a cold home. Hive Active Heating is a clever piece of kit that lets you control the temperature from a smartphone, no matter where you are. The sleek thermostat doesn't need any professional installation and will work with your existing heating system.

You can set up to six schedules a day, as well as managing the hot water. The geo-location feature also means your thermostat knows if you've gone out and left the heating on, so there's no chance of the heating blasting out into empty rooms. In fact, using a system like this means you won't have to heat an empty home again, potentially saving you up to £120 a year on heating bills. Hive, which works with any heating system, also works with Amazon Echo and Google Assistant.

◀ SONOS SPEAKERS
From £149 | sonos.com

Like the lady on the white horse, you can have music wherever you go. Or, at least, wherever you go in your home. Sonos is a wireless sound system that allows you to fill your rooms with your favourite sounds, all controlled from an app on your smart device. The system allows you to have high quality, connected speakers in as many rooms as you want. You can have the same songs playing throughout your home, or choose different tunes for different rooms. It's really easy to set up and works with all the major streaming services like Spotify, Amazon, Apple and Tidal. There's a variety of different speakers available, including the Sonos One, which works with Alexa.

ABBEYFORD LEISURE – ST ANDREWS HOLIDAY PARK

SWING BY ST ANDREWS...

... and you'll find more than just golf. New for 2020 is your chance to own your own holiday home at the new and exclusive Lade Links development at St Andrews Holiday Park

St Andrews is of "course" the home of golf; the first 18-hole course as we recognise it today was formed at the Old Course, on common land. Fascinating! And you can own a holiday home right in the heart of this historic and beautiful area, close to the oldest golf course in the world.

St Andrews Holiday Park, part of the Abbeyford Leisure group, enjoys unrivalled sea views, direct access to a beach and is only a few minutes' walk from the town of St Andrews.

Many holiday homes here offer breathtaking views without having to venture further than your window. The park is perched across the bay from St Andrews and gives owners access to everything the Fife coastline has to offer, from its golf courses to its beautifully rugged coastal walking routes.

Your entire leisure time is catered for at St Andrews Holiday Park – the site has its own bar and restaurant called The Braes. It serves a wide range from gourmet burgers to barista coffee. You can eat in the pleasant interior of the venue or take your treats outside, to the elevated sun terrace where you get one of the best views in the British Isles.

In addition, the park has its own Papa John's pizzeria takeaway.

LADE LINKS

Now, there's a new area of the park. This is an exclusive development called Lade Links. It offers hand-picked luxury holiday homes from leading manufacturers and is destined to become just as popular as St Andrews Holiday Park.

All of the pitches are spacious, with

Luxury holiday homes

The view from the park